Til COVID Do Us Part

Til COVID Do Us Part

Sarah Fischer Pointer

CONTENTS

This book is dedicated to the millions of people that we lost due to COVID 19. Also, to the medical professionals that fought on the front lines trying to save lives every day. Y'all the real deal!

Most of all, dedicated to my love, Darren, who lost his fight against COVID in March of 2020. I'll see you on the other side of the stars, my dear.

The Meeting

Who would have thought that my love story would start with the click of a mouse? I certainly wouldn't have guessed it. My name is Annie Wagner and I was twenty- seven years old when our story began. I had just moved down to Florida from Illinois with my parents a year and a half before, so I didn't really know too many local people yet and was looking to start dating again.

I clicked "Enter" and finished up my profile on *Christians Meet*. "I can't believe you convinced me to do this," I muttered to my mother, sitting beside me on the couch. "No one will ask me out on here! It's a total waste of time and money. I need to meet guys in person."

"Annie, just try it. Give it six months, and if nothing happens, you can cancel your membership. Don't worry about the cost, I'm covering it. Meet a few people on here and see what happens. If you meet 'the one,' then you meet them. If you don't, at least you can say you tried."

I shrugged and flipped through a few profiles. The first man's profile picture was taken in a gym locker room; he was holding a dumbbell in one hand and a milk jug full of water in the other. I shook my head and clicked "Next". The next profile had a vulgar screen name, so he was quickly ruled out. Then I saw the profile for "tuxxguy76." His profile picture showed a tall, lean man with dark blonde hair and blue eyes in a tuxedo.

Huh, he's pretty cute, I thought to myself. *He has a super friendly smile, and he wears glasses too.*

I clicked on the profile and his information came up. He lived in the same city in Florida as I did, and he worked in IT.

A computer nerd, I chuckled quietly. *Well, I'm pretty nerdy myself, so maybe there's a connection there? Let's see how old he is...thirty- seven? Oh, boy.*

"Here's a guy," I said to my mom, handing her my laptop. "He looks nice, but he's thirty-seven. Do you think that's too old for me? "

She looked at his photo thoughtfully and said "No, I don't think that's too old. And guys mature later than girls, so you could use an older man."

"Do men ever really reach maturity?" I quipped. My mom laughed as I took the laptop back and pondered his picture. Then a message popped up on my screen. It was from "tuxxguy76"!

Hi! He said.

Hello, I typed.

How are you?

I'm good. How are you?

Doing well, thanks. My name is Daniel.

I'm Annie. It's nice to meet you.

It's nice to meet you too. What do you do?

I'm a personal injury lawyer.

Oh, I'd better be careful then.

Smiling to myself, I answered: *"That's right, haha."*

I work in IT.

That must be interesting! What do you like to do for fun?

I love movies and music. What are your hobbies?

I love to read. Do you like Harry Potter?

Of course! I'm a Hufflepuff from way back.

"He likes *Harry Potter*!" I cried.

Mom snickered and said "A match made in heaven."

I'm either a Gryffindor or a Ravenclaw. It's kind of a toss-up.

So you're a Gryffin-claw. That's cool. Would you like to text? I can give you my number.

Sure.

We exchanged cell phone numbers and started sending texts back and forth. For a few days after that, we were virtually inseparable. We talked about our work, our families, and about our likes and dislikes. I discovered that we shared so many interests that we were virtually identical. We liked the same kinds of movies, were avid book enthusiasts (although he preferred to listen to books on audiotape while I liked to read), we both shared a love of classic rock and roll and Christian music, and we both loved cats. *He's a cat lover? That's my kind of guy!*

Above all, our Christian faith was very important to the both of us. We both regularly attended church services and, although we were not from the same denomination, we were both Protestant. Daniel had been raised Episcopalian while I was raised in the Brethren church, but we agreed that a relationship with Jesus Christ was a critical area in both our lives and that that relationship would be a foundation of any serious romantic relationship that we entered into. We were also both interested in learning more about the Jewish roots of Jesus and, by extension, of Christianity. I have strong ancestral ties to the Jewish faith, and Daniel was fascinated by my Jewish roots.

Do you want to meet in person? He asked me, three days after we first connected.

Sure, dinner or something?

Yeah, I know just the place. Meet at 7 on Friday night at Thunderstorm's for dinner and karaoke?

Karaoke, I thought, *this guy definitely knows the way to my heart.*

Can't wait, I responded to him.

Friday came more quickly that I'd expected. I got off of work at five o' clock, drove home, and changed out of my blouse and suit pants. I put on a pair of blue jeans and a pink sweater with a beach scene on it, since it was only mid- January and the nights could get a little chilly. I brushed my hair and pulled it up into a ponytail, put on a little face powder and mascara, and drove down the road to Thunderstorm, a local bar and grill. There was an outdoor patio area in front where the karaoke was set up, and several people were already sitting at tables and listening to an older gentleman belt out old love songs. I didn't see Daniel yet, so I took a seat where I could keep an eye on the parking lot. Seven o' clock came and I got a text saying: *"Sorry, I got caught in traffic. I swear I'm coming! I'll be there in 15 minutes."* I smiled.

At least he has the courtesy to let me know he's still coming!

Ok, I replied.

True to his word, ten minutes later he pulled up in his car with a bouquet of flowers. He was wearing black blue jeans and a nice polo shirt.

I went up to him and said, rather shyly, "Daniel?"

He laughed. "Yeah, and I'm guessing you're Annie?"

I smiled. "Yes, it's nice to meet you."

We hugged and I took the flowers he held out to me. "They're beautiful!"

"They're for a beautiful woman."

I breathed in the floral scent of the bouquet and motioned Daniel towards the table that I had sat at while I waited for him. We both took a seat and ordered some food and a drink. Then, we took turns singing our favorite songs and, in between, we talked and ate our meals. He sang a classic rock and roll song and I loved it. It was a song I really liked, to start with and, while he hit some off notes here and there, the joy that he radiated while singing and the song itself made me smile. I followed up with a girl- rocker song and he clapped enthusiastically for me. He put his arm around my shoulders as the night went on and the temperature started to drop.

After a few hours, I said "Well, I suppose I'd better be going home. I had a really nice time!"

"This was the best time I've had in a long time! Here, let me walk you to your car." We walked out to the parking lot, and, as I got in the driver's seat and started up my car, he handed me my purse, which I'd put on the hood of the car.

"Thanks! Definitely don't want to forget that."

"No problem." He was leaning on the driver's side of my car and poked his head through the open window to kiss me on the cheek. "I had a really fun night with you. We should do it again."

Blushing, I squeaked out "For sure!"

He squeezed my shoulder and stepped back from the car. "Send me a text when you get

home so I know you got back alright," he said, smiling.

"I will!" I answered, backing out of my parking space. I couldn't stop smiling as I saw him waving in my rearview mirror.

When I got home, I put the car in park and sat there for a second.

Got home, I texted him.

He responded immediately. *Good to hear! Want to go to the movies to-morrow night?*

Sure. What movie were you thinking?

Catching Fire sound ok?

Ok, I thought, *Hunger Games? He's asking me out on a date to see the Hunger Games?*

This is the guy for me!

Absolutely, count me in, I answered him.

Great! Pick you up at 6 for dinner?

Sounds like a plan. Where did you want to eat?

Want to eat at Friday's? It's right there by the movie theatre. They have a deal on endless apps like wings and mozzarella sticks.

That's it, I told myself, *Hunger Games and mozzarella sticks?! I'm marrying this guy.*

That sounds perfect to me, I texted back.

Our second date was just as seamless as the first. It felt like we'd known each other for years instead of just weeks. We felt completely comfortable with each other. He was a total gentleman and always knew how to make me laugh. We couldn't help but have fun together. As he dropped me off after our second date, we shared our first kiss. Although it was slightly embarrassing and awkward, as most first kisses are, it was also very sweet and heartfelt. We agreed to continue texting and to go out again the next weekend. When I got back to my computer that night, I discovered that he had sent me a relationship request on *Face and Friends*. I smiled and clicked "Accept" and, all of sudden, I was: *In a relationship with Daniel Palmer.*

After our third date, Daniel wanted to introduce me to his mother, Diane, and stepfather, Gerry. He had lived with them for a while at that point to help his mom with her medical issues. I was very nervous to meet his parents, but it went perfectly. His mother was the sweetest woman! And his stepfather was very warm and welcoming. You could tell right away how much she loved Daniel and how much he loved and respected her in return. I immediately felt like a part of the family and I knew that if Daniel treated all women like he did his mother, I was in for a treat. On our fourth date, we went bowling with my parents. That was a date most people would consider pretty lame but we actually had fun doing it. Daniel had lost his father about fifteen years before, following a prolonged illness, but he said my dad actually reminded him of his own. He said they had very similar senses of humor. I regretfully (and jokingly) told Daniel that I'd gotten my own sense of humor from my father, so there would be plenty of sarcasm in his future if he stayed with me. He laughed and said that sounded just fine to him.

Our fifth date was the weekend after that and it was actually on Valentine's Day. He sent two dozen red roses and a basket of candies and snacks to me at my office and all my female coworkers went crazy with questions. "Who is this guy?" "How old is he?" "What does he do?" "What is his name?" "How long have you been together?" "Is your relationship serious?!" After sharing some of my sweets with them, I let them know how we'd met and that I hoped our relationship was headed in a serious direction in the future.

We went to a local Caribbean themed restaurant for dinner that night and then we took a drive along the water. Sitting on the hood of his car, watching the moon reflected off the Gulf of Mexico, we held each other and talked. We talked about where we saw our lives headed in the next five to ten years, what dreams we had for ourselves, and what we hoped to accomplish in our lives. I told him that I hoped to be married in the near future and saw myself living with my husband in Florida and potentially adopting children down the road.

"I want to get married in the next few years myself," he said.

"Oh, that's good."

He nodded. "Can I tell you a secret?" he whispered.

"Sure," I whispered back.

"I think I'm in love with you."

"Can I tell *you* a secret?"

"What?"

"I think I love you too."

We kissed and just enjoyed the balmy evening together before we stopped at his favorite ice cream parlor on the way back to my house. He dropped me off and then went home himself. That whole spring season pretty much passed like that. We exchanged "good morning" texts every day. We continued to text throughout the day, making random jokes or commenting about our day. We tagged each other in funny memes on *Face and Friends.* There were consistent "good night" texts. We shared lots of "I love you" texts. Our weekends always included dinner followed by an activity like a movie or karaoke and a long drive. Every Friday and Saturday night that spring, we had effortless dates that were fun yet romantic.

Summer of that year came fast and furious. Florida summers are always brutal, of course, but it felt hotter and more humid that year. When the Fourth of July holiday arrived, Daniel arranged for my parents, his mother and stepfather and the both of us to have dinner at Fisherman's Wharf. It was a very nice restaurant right on the water and we sat in an open area overlooking the Caloosahatchee River. We enjoyed a fantastic dinner and then the fireworks show started. They were being shot off from a bridge nearby, and I was mesmerized by the fireworks and their light reflected on the water. Suddenly, Daniel tugged at my sleeve and, when I turned to look at him, he was down on one knee.

"Annie, I love you. I know we've only been together for six months but I also know that we're right for each other. I want to spend forever with you. Will you marry me?"

I gasped and then goggled at the diamond ring he was holding in a white ring box in his hand. I nodded mutely, tears springing to my eyes. "Yes," I murmured. "Yes, I will!" As he slipped the ring on my finger, the fireworks continued to go off and we kissed while our parents cheered. All the other diners around us started to shout and clap as they figured out what had happened. A waitress brought us a complimentary slice of cake to celebrate, and we took lots of pictures. Daniel and my dad even posed for a photo shaking hands, which made me feel slightly like a piece of chattel. The smiles on both of their faces made me smile, though.

We were engaged! As he drove me home that evening, the time had come to discuss our future living arrangements. I had purchased a single family home two years before, with my parents as co- signers, and I wasn't sure that my parents could afford to pay the mortgage and keep up the house on their own. Surprisingly, Daniel wasn't opposed to them living with us! He completely understood my desire to make sure that they were taken care of, and since the house had three bedrooms and two bathrooms, we would have our own dedicated space.

My mom and I had previously scheduled a trip to Universal Studios in Orlando for the end of July, and we all figured that would be a good time for Daniel to move in to the house. We cleared the guest room and he moved his bed, desk, dresser and personal belongings (with some help from my dad and Gerry) into the house while we were gone. When I got back from vacation, I suddenly had a fiancée living with me! It was amazing. It took a little getting used to, suddenly having four fully grown adults in the house, but it worked out pretty well. My parents took the master suite while we had the second largest bedroom and the main bathroom all to ourselves. We were head over heels in love and adored getting to share a home together. The four of us settled into a happy routine.

Monday through Friday, my mother worked at a factory while I worked at a law office. Daniel was working with an IT firm full time as well, so the three of us were gone pretty much all day during the work week. We'd typically come together for dinner around six o' clock, where we'd sit in front of the TV in the family room and eat over an episode of *Seinfeld*. We'd trade jokes and commentary about our day. ("How was your day today? Was it a good day today or a bad day today?") Then we'd watch the nightly news followed by some kind of game show that we all liked (*Jeopardy* or something similar) before the guys split off and went back to the bedrooms to relax. Mom and I would watch *The Bachelor* or some other show we liked and we'd all go to bed around nine thirty or ten o' clock.

Daniel and I developed our own bedtime routine. He would already be lying down and watching *The Simpsons* when I came into the bedroom around ten o' clock, and I'd bring the dog in with me. I'd lay the dog down beside him, get in my pajamas, brush my teeth and then we'd just lay in bed and talk. The dog would borrow down under the blankets and cuddle with us. If Daniel's legs or feet were particularly cramped from a long day of work, I'd give him a massage. If my back was really sore from sitting in a desk chair for nine hours straight, he'd give me a massage. Then he'd turn out the lights, and we'd fall asleep snuggled up together.

On Saturday mornings, my mom and I would run errands and do the grocery shopping while Daniel did laundry and dad did yard work. On either Friday or Saturday nights, we'd typically do something as a family one night (rent a movie, play a board game, etc.), and the other night would be just for Daniel and I. We would go to the movies, go out and do karaoke with some friends, grab dinner, or just go for a long drive along the coast. No matter what we did together, it was always fun. Those first years that Daniel and I were together have to be, without a doubt, the happiest years of my entire life. I will never forget them.

Daniel and I got along so well because we were both big, goofy kids at heart. A good example of how well we meshed is the song "Love is an

Open Door," from *Frozen*. When Anna and the prince are singing the song together, they finish each other sentences, saying the same things and dancing perfectly in unison without any rehearsal. That was basically how our relationship was, we were always in sync. With just one look, we could immediately know what the other was thinking. Daniel would put the *Frozen* soundtrack on in his car and we would both sing our parts at the top of our lungs, laughing together at any sour notes that we hit. At the end of the song, we would always put our hands together, fingers curved to form one half of a heart. That was a good metaphor for how it felt to be with Daniel: like I had found a puzzle piece I didn't even know was missing from my life and, when I was with him, I was suddenly whole.

The only bone of contention between us, as the saying goes, was housekeeping. I quickly realized that, while I was very organized and tidy, Daniel tended to leave things lying around on the floor and didn't really like to clean. Although I sometimes complained to him about it, I typically tried to let the issue go. While we had some verbal arguments about household chores over the course of our relationship, I would say only two or three of those arguments were ever really heated. Most of the time, we were like two peas in a pod.

2

The Wedding

After the Fourth of July proposal, it was time to plan our wedding. First, we needed to choose a date. The summer isn't a great time to have a wedding in Florida because it's so hot and rainy outside, so we didn't even consider it. Winter was also not an option, since Christmas, Hanukkah and the New Year would keep many of our out of town family and friends from being able to attend. Spring wouldn't really work either because that was only six to eight months away, which I didn't think gave us enough time to plan. That only left the fall, which was already my favorite season. September can still be very hot in South Florida, and both of our birthdays and Thanksgiving fell in November, so we decided that mid- October was the best.

After choosing a wedding date, the financial aspects of the wedding were the biggest concern. We discussed it for a while and agreed that Daniel and I would pay for the wedding ourselves, out of the little bit of savings that we had and our current incomes. Thankfully, we both had very good jobs at that time and were making decent incomes, so, with mom and dad helping to pay the household bills, we still had a fair amount of disposable income left at the end of each month. Both of us agreed that we could afford to split a wedding budget of ten thousand dollars in total, so we went about planning a wedding that fit into that budget.

Choosing a venue for the ceremony was the easiest part. Since our faith was so important to us, we knew that we wanted a church ceremony. At that time, we were attending a Nazarene church so we booked the church's sanctuary for our wedding date and ensured that the pastor could officiate. We were amazed to find that we wouldn't be charged for the use of the sanctuary for our wedding and, even better, we got a free pre- marital class with our pastor! The church was such a blessing to us both before and after our wedding. When it came to the reception, though, a venue was harder to come by. If we wanted to have food and dancing at the reception, we couldn't have it inside the church. There was really no outdoor area at the church where we could set up a tent for the reception either, so we started looking around for a reception venue.

We looked at a few nearby churches for the reception, but it didn't make sense to change from one church for the ceremony to another church for the reception, so we decided to go with a non- religious venue for the reception. After researching the community center and several banquet halls and hotels, along with their prices and catering policies, we decided a marina and hotel downtown offered the best price (in addition to hotel rooms for the bridal party and set up and clean up services!). Everything was starting to come together. I left Daniel in charge of his own tux and the groomsmen's attire and turned my attention to finding my dream wedding dress.

My first step, sans fiancée, was a bridal salon. I went to try on dresses on a bright and sunny Saturday morning with my mother and Diane in tow. Being as short as I am, it can be pretty difficult to find dresses that fit me properly. However, the saleswoman that handled my dress fitting appointment was sure that she could find me the right dress. I told her that I wished to spend no more than four hundred dollars on my dress, so she brought out three of them that were in that price range. The first one was just a long, plain, straight cut dress that looked more like a prom dress than a wedding dress. I shook my head and didn't even try it on.

The second dress was lacey with lots of frills and a very full skirt. I tried it on and stepped out of the dressing room. I looked at myself and the mirror for a second and cried out "I look like a cupcake!" My mom and mother in law both shook their heads in the mirror behind me so I ducked back into the dressing room. The saleswoman unzipped the dress for me and said "I think I may have just the dress. It might be a little bit over your price range, though."

"How far over my price range is it?" I asked cautiously.

"It's priced at five hundred dollars, marked down from eight hundred."

I hesitated. "I guess I'll give it a try..."

She took the dress and left the room, returning a few minutes later with the most beautiful dress I had ever seen. It was long and white, strapless, with gorgeous lacework and pearls across the bodice and the hem. When I tried the dress on, it was absolutely perfect. I had wanted straps or cap sleeves to hold the dress up more securely, but the saleswoman assured me that they could sew special cups into the bodice to ensure that, even though it was strapless, it wouldn't fall down. I stepped out of the dressing room and looked in the mirror. I felt like a fairy tale princess! I started to tear up and looked behind me in the mirror to see my mother and Diane crying as well. We all laughed at the same time and said "That's the one!"

"It's a little expensive," I whispered to my mom. "It's five hundred dollars."

She pursed her lips together for a moment before answering "Well, that's only one hundred more than you originally planned on spending. And it's a special occasion! You only get married once."

She hugged me tightly. "Hopefully," I chuckled.

The dress had to be hemmed, of course, because it was too long, but I absolutely loved it. It was taken to alterations and, as we walked up to the cash register to purchase the dress, my mother surprised me by insisting that she was covering the cost! She and my father couldn't help much with the wedding, but they wanted to buy the dress for me as part of their gift to us. The three of us left the store exhausted but grinning from ear to ear.

Next, we had to deal with the wedding flowers. Luckily, Diane was a member of the local Garden Club and had floral connections for days (in addition to being extremely talented in doing floral arrangements!).

We literally didn't have to worry about any of the floral details. She just asked us what our wedding colors were and got together with the rest of the Garden Club members and they made all the arrangements. Of course, once an arrangement was completed, Diane would send me a picture of it for final approval, but other than that we had zero worries in the flower department. On top of that, Diane, Gerry, and the Garden Club graciously covered the cost of the flowers as well, which was a real lifesaver.

We also needed to choose wedding colors for our flowers, décor and the formal wear that the bridal party would be wearing. Daniel was a huge Florida Gators fan, so he was in favor of orange and blue. I vetoed that right away, insisting that orange was not a wedding color. My favorite colors were purple and pink, but Daniel immediately said no to the pink. He thought pink was too feminine. Daniel was alright with purple, though, which worked well because Diane said that purple and white would make fantastic colors for floral arrangements. So, purple and white became our official wedding colors. Now I had to choose bridesmaids dresses.

On another bright and sunny Saturday morning, I took three of my local girlfriends and my mom and mother in law and we hit the bridal salon to look at bridesmaid's dresses. I knew that I wanted an ankle length dress in purple, so we looked at the color swatches that they had at the salon and I picked a royal purple. My girlfriends looked at different dresses, tried on a few of them, and eventually chose a straight cut, strapless ball gown that would look good on all of them. We ordered the dresses and I let my out of town best friends know which dress we'd chosen so that they could order a matching dress from their local bridal salon.

Since we'd chosen the location for the reception, which permitted us to bring in our own catering, we started to shop around for caterers. A lot of the caterers that we found were super pricey and didn't fit into the catering budget we'd allocated for ourselves. We decided that, since our favorite cakes always came from a local supermarket deli, we would have our cake and our catering come from there. We chose several different platters of shrimp, sandwiches, finger foods and fruit for our guests to choose from and taste tested several cakes before choosing a chocolate cake with strawberry inside that would be decorated with faux seashells.

About three months prior to the wedding, it came time to choose our Save the Date cards and wedding invitations. Daniel and I, along with both of our mothers, calculated that we needed to invite around two hundred people all together, although we only expected around one hundred to actually attend. We went to a local card shop and looked at their selection of invitations. Since we live on the Gulf Coast, I figured that a nautical theme for both the Save the Date cards and the invitations would be neat. Daniel agreed with the nautical theme and we chose some cards and invitations in our price range and ordered them right away.

Last but certainly not least, we needed to figure out what kind of décor we were going to use for our reception. Continuing with the nautical theme, I researched tropical wedding décor and found a really neat idea involving mason jars, sand, tea light candles and seashells that I thought would make a really neat centerpiece for the reception tables. My mom and I were putting these centerpieces together for several days, and my mother in law even added some floral décor to the mix that worked well with the sand and seashells. Daniel and I chose a cake topper with a happy couple on a sandy beach and I made a table skirt for the bridal party's table that looked like a grass skirt.

For the wedding favors, we purchased tiny purple gift bags and put a small champagne bottle of bubbles in each of them. We even added a few personalized details that we bought online in bulk. We bought mint tins with a beach scene on them that had our names and our wedding date stamped on them, and some seashell magnets for the guests to take home. The centerpieces and favor bags required so many seashells that, to this day, we still have a huge box full of them in our hall closet!

Not everyone has a bachelor or bachelorette party, of course, and parties for Daniel and I were a little difficult considering that my two best friends lived in the Midwest and one of his best friends lived several hours north of us. We decided to make the best of it, though, and Daniel's brother planned a bachelor party a few weeks before our wedding including dinner and a trip to a local brewery with a few of the guys. Daniel was a big fan of craft beer, and absolutely loved his bachelor party. My mom and I planned a trip downtown that included dinner and drinks with a few of my local girlfriends and my mother and sister in law. They were very low- key parties, but we loved them so much and were so grateful to the people that could attend.

Gifts for the bridal party members were fairly easy to choose, and we bought them a few weeks before the wedding. I decided to buy a necklace with the first letter of their names on it for each of my bridesmaids, and Daniel went with an engraved beer stein for each of his groomsmen. We couldn't talk about what we were going to get each other for the big day, of course, and I had a very hard time thinking of something to get Daniel. I mentioned it to one of my best friends, who got married just four months before I did, and she told me that she had gotten her husband a personalized book called *Why I Love You*. I thought that was a great idea and I liked that it allowed you to write notes and store important little mementos inside the book, so I got Daniel a *Why I Love You* book for our wedding day and got busy personalizing it.

Just before the wedding, we had to choose wedding bands. We went to the same local jeweler that Daniel had purchased my engagement ring from and decided on matching white gold bands (a band with diamonds in it for me, a plain band for Daniel) that were in our price range. We would be paying off the cost of our wedding for several months afterwards, but we didn't mind. We were planning our dream wedding on a budget, and we were so excited for it. Not to toot our own horns, but it can be pretty hard to plan a whole wedding, a reception for one hundred people, and a honeymoon, all for less than ten thousand dollars!

The night before the wedding, we had the rehearsal dinner. Luckily, that dinner is the purview of the groom's family, so it was one less thing for me to worry about. We had the dinner at a local restaurant that shut down early just so we could have our private party. It was a delicious dinner and it made us so happy to be surrounded by our family and closest friends. My two best friends even flew in from the Midwest for it! Daniel picked them up from the airport and drove them to the marina and hotel where our reception was going to be held. After I got off of work, I went to the marina and picked them up for the dinner. I hadn't seen them for a few months so, of course, we had to squeal and jump up and down like maniacs when we reunited. It was already getting cool out up north, so the girls were very excited to be in sunny Florida.

After the rehearsal dinner, the girls and I headed down to the beach. The sun was going down and we walked along the boardwalk, catching up and gossiping. They went out into the water a little ways, up to their calves, and started splashing each other. I just laughed at their touristy behavior and told them that, since I was a proper Floridian now, the water was "too cold" for me to go in. Then we stopped by a beach bar and had a drink. I was wearing my "bride to be" sash and my two best friends were telling everyone in the bar "Hey! Look! Our best friend is getting married!" I was blushing as red as a radish, but at least I got a free drink for my embarrassment.

Then we headed back to the marina hotel where I would stay the night with them. Their bed was only a double, and while the two insisted that we could all squish in together, I decided to sleep on the floor. Thanks to my dad, I inherited the ability to sleep just about anywhere, so I took a few pillows and a blanket and wrapped myself up into a "bridal burrito" on the floor beside their bed. We stayed up late that night, talking about how much we missed each other and how married life was treating the one of us that was already married. My two best friends had my "second bachelorette party" one of the best times of my life.

The next morning, the more outgoing of my two best friends shook me and said "Wake up!"

I grunted in response, burying my head under the pillow.

"It's your wedding day!"

Just like Anna in *Frozen* on coronation day, I poked my head up (bed head and all) out of the blankets and said "Wedding day!?"

The two laughed and we went down to the marina hotel lobby to get our complimentary breakfast. I was sitting at the table with them, eating a bowl of cereal, when we saw Daniel walking past the hotel lobby. I put my hand up to wave at him but one of my friends quickly pushed my head under the table.

"Hey!" I protested.

"He can't see you before the wedding! It'll bring bad luck!" she cried.

Before the wedding, we had our matron of honor and best man give us each our wedding gifts that we had picked out for each other. Daniel gave me my favorite expensive perfume, which smelled wonderful. I made sure to put a splash of it on my neck and both of my wrists before the ceremony. It was time to do our hair and makeup. We had a hairdresser and a couple of her assistants scheduled to do all of the bridesmaids' hair and makeup (five girls all together) at the marina hotel, in addition to both mothers and, of course, my own hair and makeup. We started at 8 A.M. and, by 3 P.M., I was the only one left with her hair and makeup undone. By the time they were finished with my subtle makeup and my updo, topped with my mother's veil, it was 4 P.M. We were late!

Everyone else was already dressed, but I was still wearing a button up shirt and jeans as we rushed to the church. After making sure that Daniel was nowhere to be seen, I was rushed into the church feeling like I had more security than the President himself. We holed up in the church library and prepared to get my dress on. After stripping down to my bra and underwear, I remembered "I need to go to the bathroom!"

"What?!" my mom cried.

"Before I get my dress on, I should go to the bathroom!"

She groaned and yelled out into to the hall for the other girls to make sure that no one was out there so I could come out. After getting the signal that the coast was clear, mom ushered me next door to the bathroom in my underclothes. I felt ridiculous, running down the church hallway half naked, but no one saw me. After going to the bathroom, I rushed back to the library and was helped on with my dress. I got my stockings and white flats on and we hurried out to the church lobby. The brides-maids slowly made their way down the aisle as my parents and I waited around the corner.

The wedding march began, and that was my cue.

"Ready?" my dad asked.

I nodded. "Ready."

We rounded the corner, stood in the doorway of the sanctuary for a moment, and started to proceed down the aisle. My mom was one side of me, and my dad was on the other. I could see Daniel at the end of the long aisle, beaming at me. He looked so handsome in his black tux. I beamed back and choked back tears. *I never thought this day would come!* My parents walked me up to Daniel and responded "We do" when the preacher asked who was giving me away. They each kissed me on the cheek and hugged me before sitting down.

I don't remember many specifics about the actual ceremony, to be honest, except for the fact that we used traditional vows and our own personalized vows (Daniel sang his, of course). What I remember most, though, is Daniel standing in front of me, holding my hands, and smil-ing. He was smiling so big, he was so happy. He was even tearing up, which made me tear up more. I also remember that, when it came time to place the rings on each other's fingers, Daniel's wouldn't fit. I tried unsuccessfully to shove the ring on his finger, but he whispered "Don't!" With a jerk of his head, he nodded towards my father. I looked at my parents quizzically but they both shook their heads.

I looked at the ring more closely. *Weird,* I thought. *This doesn't look right.* I let it go for the moment and placed the ring on his pinkie finger instead. Daniel put the ring on my finger, we both said "I do," and the pastor pronounced us man and wife. Daniel tipped me back and kissed me enthusiastically as the whole church cheered. The music started and we processed down the aisle in order. I remember standing out in the church lobby, receiving everyone's congratulations. I remember lots of hugs, and lots o smiles. Several people from our church back in Illinois had even traveled to see us married.

My mother came up to me at one point and I said "What was wrong with the ring?!"

She laughed. "That was your dad's ring!"

"What are you talking about?!"

"We forgot Daniel's in the library! And the door locked behind us when we closed it! We'll have to have the pastor unlock the library before we leave the church so we can get it."

"No wonder it wouldn't fit right!"

We laughed so much about that. It was the first in a series of mishaps that did nothing to dampen our joy on that day. After that, we went back into the sanctuary and took photos. Luckily, Daniel's friend was a professional photographer and agreed to do our pictures for free as our wedding gift. What a budget saver! We did photos of the whole wedding party. Then we took shots of just the bride and bridesmaids. Photos of the groom and groomsmen came next. Then we took family photos, the Wagners going first, followed by the Palmers. Finally, we took pictures of just the bride and groom.

Following the photo session, it was time to head to the reception. We carpooled to the marina hotel and waited outside until the deejay announced us all. Fortunately, another one of Daniel's friends agreed to be the deejay that night and he announced the names of the wedding party as they entered to great applause. Finally, it was time for "Mr. and Mrs. Daniel Palmer!"

We ran out on to the patio area where the reception was set up, arms held victoriously in the air. A few people gave some speeches as we shared a champagne toast. We had appetizers (fruit and shrimp platters) and then we had our first dance. We had worked out a simple choreography to John Legend's "All of Me", and it was a great first dance. However, the sound system became the second in our series of wedding glitches. Daniel's deejay friend had a sound system that was intended for indoor use, and it could barely be heard in the outdoor patio area where our reception was being held unless you were right in front of the speakers. We made the best of it and then did our father- daughter and mother- son dances. My dad and I danced to "My Girl," and it was a very special moment.

Then, it was time to cut the cake. We had already agreed not to shove cake in each other's faces, so we just nicely fed a small bit of cake to each other and pieces of cake were doled out to the guests. The third and biggest of our wedding mishaps happened next. When planning for the catering, I had ordered enough platters for up to one hundred people. I would guess that around fifty to seventy- five people were at our reception in total, and so we should have had more than enough food for everyone. I checked the total number of platters that the deli was supposed to deliver, and they were short by at least three. Everyone got to eat, in the end, but only a little bit and not exactly as I had planned.

I started to tear up at the bridal party table when I discovered that the food was wrong, and Daniel tried to console me. He put his arm around me and said "If they came for the food, they came for the wrong reasons."

"Well, that's true, I guess."

"In the end, all that matters is that we got married."

He squeezed my hand and I smiled and squeezed his back.

After a little bit of dancing, the guests started to head out. The wedding party decided to walk just down the street to the downtown area for some drinks, since we hadn't been able to afford an open bar. So we all went downtown in our wedding attire and had a drink. There must have been some sort of event going on that night, because the downtown area was very busy. Everyone complimented our dresses and tuxes and we soon headed back to the marina hotel.

Mom helped me out of my wedding dress and Daniel and I retired to our bridal suite for the night. We were married! It was hard to believe, but we were actually married. Our wedding night was very special, but I'm afraid that if you're looking for specific details, you're barking up the wrong tree. I'll leave the rest up to your imagination.

The morning after, we had a little brunch with the bridal party out on the marina hotel patio. We had muffins and croissants and coffee and juice and we all talked about how beautiful and fun the wedding was. My two best friends, sadly, had to fly back to the Midwest that day and Daniel drove them to the airport for me as my mother and I loaded up our dresses and wedding gifts into our vehicle to take home.

We carefully cataloged all of our wedding gifts and I made sure to send out thank you cards. In fact, I think I had all of the thank you cards mailed within about one week of the wedding itself, which isn't bad. I went to Social Security with a copy of our marriage certificate and ordered a new Social Security card that read "Annie Wagner Palmer," and went to the DMV to get a new driver's license with my new name on it as well. To complete the process, I filed a copy of the marriage certificate with our County Clerk's office and it was legally official: I was a married woman. We settled into married life and started to pack for our honeymoon, which was scheduled for early November.

I showed my new driver's license to Daniel and said "Well, it's official now, you're mine to annoy forever."

He laughed. "Oh, is that right? Forever, you say?"

"I'm afraid so," I said with mock solemnity. "I thought you realized, I don't believe in divorce. There are no returns at this store, I'm afraid. You're stuck with me now."

He wrapped his arms around me and murmured "There's no one else in this world that I would rather be stuck with."

3

The Honeymoon(s)

As hard as it was for me to believe, Daniel, a lifelong Florida resident, had never been on a cruise before. "You live two hours from one of the largest cruise ports in the world, and you've never been on a cruise?!" I cried.

"No," he said thoughtfully. "I mean, I've been on lots of boats before, but never a cruise ship. Why?"

"Cruising is the ultimate all- inclusive vacation! You're never going to be able to get lodging, transportation, food, and entertainment for the price that you'll get a cruise." I exclaimed. "That settles it; we're going on a cruise for our honeymoon! I've been cruising every other year since I was nine years old. It's time you got hooked on cruising, too!"

I booked us a five day honeymoon cruise and we got away with only paying a little over a thousand dollars total for the trip, which was a steal. We each took the week off of work and we packed a large suitcase full of tropical clothing, swimwear and formal evening wear. I made sure to pack a few books and we packed our cell phone chargers, toiletries and medications and we were ready to go. Daniel had introduced me to many different places, museums, restaurants and bars around Southwest Florida in our time together, so it was refreshing when I actually got to introduce him to something new. My parents drove us to the dockyard in Miami and dropped us off. After some hugs and tearful goodbyes, we headed into the terminal to embark on our ship.

Just as I'd predicted, Daniel got hooked on cruising right off the bat. It was so great getting to see how blown away he was by every aspect of our vacation. There were so many things that I no longer really noticed, after several cruises, but they were all new and exciting to him. "The ship is huge!" "Look at the elegant furniture in the lobby!" They have glass elevators where you can see the entire lobby as you go up and down!" "There are two pools!?" "Our room is huge!" *He must have expected a closet,* I thought to myself, *because the rooms were still fairly small.* "Room service is included!? You mean, I can get lobster at 2 A.M. if I want to?" I just laughed because seeing his eyes light up and his huge smile as he discovered things on the ship was like seeing a kid opening toys on Christmas morning.

Our honeymoon cruise was made even more special by how far out of their way the crew went to make sure that we enjoyed ourselves. Since we were on our honeymoon, we were greeted with special "Happy Honeymoon" decorations in our cabin, along with champagne and chocolate covered strawberries (*Thanks, moms!*). The captain even sent us personalized champagne glasses to keep, along with a little note congratulating us on our nuptials. And it seemed like everywhere we went, the crew spoiled us. "Congratulations!" "Happy Honeymoon!" "What can we do to make your trip better?" "It's your honeymoon! Have a free drink coupon!"

We didn't have to pay for a single drink on that cruise, and we even had free drinks coupons to spare at the end of it. Daniel and I quickly fell into a relaxing cruise routine. He'd always tended to wake up earlier than I did and he would go to the dining room each morning by himself for a full breakfast. I would wake up a little later, and Daniel would usually be back in our cabin by then. I would order myself some breakfast from room service and would take my time getting ready for the day. Around ten o' clock (if it was a sea day), we'd go up to the pool deck. We would swim together, relax in the hot tub, lounge by the pool and talk, or read a book. We soaked up the sunshine and then, when lunchtime came, we'd eat poolside.

After lunch, we'd usually enjoy whatever activity was taking place on the pool deck that day. There were trivia games, dancing competitions, hairy chest contests, and other fun things. Sometimes we joined in, but most of the time we just watched and laughed. We did win Harry Potter Trivia one day though, hands down. Our prize for winning the trivia was a little plastic model cruise ship on a stick. We would head back to our cabin for a couple of hours before dinner, enjoy a little "honeymoon time" before showering and getting dressed for the evening. We always had dinner in the main dining room. Daniel poked fun at me for eating from the kid's menu, but honestly, all the food was delicious. We quickly made friends with our "bread guy," our waiter, our "water guy," and the rest of the dining staff as they bent over backwards to make sure that we had whatever food we wanted. Daniel exclaimed at the dining options most of all: "Sirloin Steak?! And it's included?!" and we always ate our fill. After dinner, we'd take in a show in the main theatre, enjoying the spectacular singing and dancing.

And then we'd do our favorite activity of all: cruise karaoke. We'd sing solos and duets, and chat with our fellow singers at the bar. We even joined in a karaoke contest! The karaoke contest was, honestly, one of the best moments of my whole life. I will never forget it. Nine of the best acts from our cruise karaoke nights were invited to sing on the big stage in the main theater, backed up by a real live band. And Daniel and I made the cut! We were invited to perform and we chose our song, which was "Don't Stop Believing," by Journey. Daniel and I made sure we cleaned up and dressed nicely for the occasion. I remember I had on a short black dress with spaghetti straps and little black sandals and he was wearing black slacks and a button down shirt with black dress shoes.

We were the last act to go on stage, so we had a lot of time on our hands. Sitting in the front row, waiting, I was incredibly nervous. Daniel ordered a cup of coffee for himself and encouraged me to sip a little bit of it. "But I don't like coffee," I reminded him.

"I know, but the warmth will help loosen up your vocal chords!"

I took a sip of the coffee, and it really did help soothe my throat and made me feel more prepared to sing. When our turn came up, we were ushered backstage. We were each given a microphone and, with the band behind us, the curtains rose. There was a moment of silence where I felt my stomach quiver with anticipation. Daniel took my hand and squeezed it reassuringly. The music started and we broke out in song. The theater was completely full that night, and as soon as we started singing the audience went wild. They all stood up and sang along, swaying with the beat and waving their hands. We each worked our way up and down one side of the stage as we sang our parts and played to the crowd. Finally, the last few chords of the song rang out as Daniel and I met in the middle of the stage, clasped hands, raised them above our heads, and sang "Don't Stop!"

The audience was cheering and shouting like crazy, but we didn't end up winning the contest. It didn't matter, though, because we still felt like we had won. We hugged each other tightly and sat back down in the front row to applaud the winner. I'll never forget the feeling of his hand in mine, and what felt like our souls connecting as we lifted our hands and voices in song. I'll never forget how happy we were to be there and, more importantly, to be together.

I don't remember all of the ports of call that we stopped at during our honeymoon trip, but I remember that one of them was Grand Turk. This had been one of my favorite ports of call since I'd first visited it years ago and it was amazing to see Daniel discover Grand Turk for the first time. "The water here is so blue!" he cried, surprised that the water wasn't a dull greenish- brown like the Gulf back home. He admired all the little shops and the music that was playing as we walked down the boardwalk. We sat by the pool together at Margaritaville and enjoyed a burger, French fries, and a margarita while Daniel told me the story of how he had met Jimmy Buffett in person at a Margaritaville in Key West years before.

That honeymoon did not feel long enough, and Daniel insisted that we take another cruise together soon. We repacked our suitcase and we both had tears in our eyes as we waved sadly at the ship after disembarking. My parents picked us up at the dockyard and we told them about our trip the whole ride home. Sadly, of course, after our honeymoon, we each had to go back to work. We re- settled into our happy family routine and everything was good for a time.

It was around six months to a year after our wedding that we decided to take a "second honeymoon" to Universal Studios in Orlando. Daniel had been to Universal before, but hadn't been back in years and had never gotten to see The Wizarding World of Harry Potter, which they'd recently added to the park. We booked a hotel near Universal for two nights and packed for a long weekend away. After checking into the hotel and dropping off our luggage, we headed to the park. We paid the parking fee, found a parking spot, and waited in line to get into the park.

"You know what originally attracted me to you, right?" I asked him.

"My dashing good looks?" he asked, running his hand through his hair.

I laughed. "Yes, of course. I was referring to something besides that, though."

He thought for a moment. "Was it my dazzling wit?"

"Oh, definitely. But, overall, you had me at 'I like *Harry Potter*,'" I giggled.

"Well, I'm glad I told you, then," he chuckled.

We got through the gates after going through security and we walked around the park, talking and taking lots of pictures. One of my favorite photos was a shot of the two of us in front of the Universal ball. I also got some funny photos of Daniel in *The Simpsons* area as well, where he struck a pose like "Duff Man" next to the statute of the character. We went on a bunch of rides, got a soda and snacks to share, and just enjoyed the beautiful early December weather. My absolute favorite part of that trip, though, was watching Daniel's face as we entered Diagon Alley for the first time. We rounded the corner and came upon a whole area of stores and restaurants that looked like they were straight out of the *Harry Potter* movies.

"Wow!" He gasped. "There are real cobblestones on this street! And look at all the decorations in the store windows. The stores look just like the books describe them!"

He wanted to buy a wand in Diagon Alley, but I told him "You should wait to get a wand at Ollivander's! It's a whole experience. We can do that tomorrow when we go across to the other part of the park."

We finished touring Diagon Alley before leaving the park for the day. The next morning, each wearing our favorite House gear, we took the Hogwarts Express across the park to Hogsmeade and Daniel was just as shocked by how realistic the little town and Hogwarts Castle looked. We stood in line and waited for about a half hour before we were admitted to Ollivander's Wand Shop. Luckily, it was another beautiful day outside and wasn't too hot.

Once inside the dark little shop, the middle aged wizard behind the counter chose a child to wave different wands around until he found the right one. My first trip to Universal, a few years before, had gone pretty much the same way and, even though the wizard had tried to usher my mom and I out of the shop after the chosen child had his wand experience, I had insisted that I also be given the chance to have a wand choose me. After all, we'd waited for three hours in the blazing July sun that day to find the right wand!

This trip, I took the wizard behind the counter aside and told him that we were on our honeymoon and Daniel had never gotten the chance to have a wand to choose him before. I begged the man to let Daniel do the wand experience, and he graciously agreed. Daniel stood in front of the counter and was handed three wands, one right after the other. The first two wands made things go wrong around the shop, and the wizard said that those definitely weren't meant for Daniel. The third wand made a bright light shine right on Daniel and heavenly music play in the background. Daniel had found his wand. Seeing the delight on his face as his wand chose him made the whole trip worthwhile and I was lucky enough to capture the moment on video.

We went through a door to the gift shop and found the size and style of wand that had chosen Daniel and, to our surprise, they were electronic. They hadn't had those types of wands when I'd done the experience years before. These new wands had some sort of electronic sensor in them that made things happen around the park when you waved them correctly! It was truly magical and fun for the both of us to find spots in the park to use his wand, and to try to wave them correctly to activate them. Almost as if the wand truly had chosen Daniel, it seemed to work better for him than it did for me. We had lunch at the Three Broomsticks, went on a few more rides, walked around the *Jurassic Park* area, and then started our three hour drive back home. How I wish we could have one more day together at Universal now!

Soon after our second honeymoon, Daniel and I started attending a new non- denominational Christian church around the corner from our house. We would attend church service and then, during the church service after that, I would serve in the pre- school room with the little kids while Daniel served in the early elementary room with the school kids. The pastors of that church were fantastic and we loved the kids and the volunteers that we got to serve with. Our service with the children's ministry got us both thinking about children of our own.

Approximately six months after our honeymoon, I had a routine appointment with my cardiologist. I was devastated to discover that, while it may be possible for me to get pregnant, it wasn't really advisable that I carry a pregnancy to term. I went home and gave Daniel the bad news with tears in my eyes. He held me as I cried and told me "I didn't just marry you because I wanted a baby! I married you because I love you."

I insisted that we could still try to have a baby and that I was willing to take the risk, but he shook his head immediately. "No," he said. "No. I waited thirty seven years to find you. I am not going to take any risk of losing you. If we really want to have kids, we can adopt, or we can foster. There are lots of ways to become a parent." I loved him even more for his comforting words and, even though I felt very sad that I couldn't give him a child of his own, I was overwhelmed by the unconditional love that he showed me.

We started looking into private adoption, but quickly found that it was way too expensive for us. Our research uncovered that it could cost anywhere from thirty to sixty thousand dollars to adopt a baby through a private organization, and that was just the adoption itself! On top of that, you had to consider the cost of raising a child to age eighteen, which was astronomical. We then looked into the possibility of surrogacy, but that was just as expensive and difficult as the process of private adoption. Moreover, we both had genetic issues that we were fearful would be passed on to a baby, so we decided that a baby that was biologically ours wasn't a good idea.

Our last possible route to parenthood was foster parenting, and we were hoping to turn our third bedroom into a bedroom for a child. Foster parenting classes were being offered in the town next to ours and for eight weeks we drove thirty five minutes each way to attend a two hour class in foster care. The class was very enlightening and we met some wonderful people along the way, but we eventually decided that it was not for us. We became certified as foster parents but a work related accident that Daniel suffered set off a whole series of medical problems that made it clear that we wouldn't have the money, time, or good health to care for a child. The honeymoon phase of our relationship ended at that point, and the difficult phase began.

4

The Difficult Phase

Around six months after our honeymoon, Daniel dropped a heavy object onto his foot while he was working. While this wouldn't usually pose too much of a problem for a person with no pre- existing medical conditions, Daniel was a diabetic. His diabetes didn't normally cause many issues, as he took insulin for it on a daily basis and had his blood sugar pretty well under control.

Unfortunately, with diabetes often comes diabetic neuropathy, and Daniel's feet and hands were slowly losing sensation. Because he had such bad neuropathy, Daniel hadn't even realized how badly he'd hurt his foot until he started having issues with his toe. Two days after his accident I noticed when he pulled off his socks and shoes that his big toe was completely black.

"What happened?" I cried.

"I dropped something on it at work. Don't worry, it doesn't hurt too much," he explained. I insisted that he needed to get it looked at right away. It was late at night by that point and I had to go to work in the morning, so my dad agreed to take Daniel to the ER close to our house. I told him I'd leave my cell phone on and lying next to me in bed if he needed me.

Around midnight, he called me to tell me that they were going to have to amputate his toe. I immediately got up and rushed to the hospital to be with him. I held his hand and tried to comfort him as much as I could until his mother arrived later that morning. I called off work that day and went to bed for a few hours before coming back to the ER.

By that time, Daniel had been admitted to the hospital and had his own room, and the operation was planned for the next day. I called my supervisor and let him know I would need off of work the next day, too. I was allowed to stay with Daniel in the pre- surgical area until they were ready to take him to the operating room, and I tried to be as encouraging as possible. This was his very first surgery, so he was incredibly nervous about being put under anesthesia and there were tears in his eyes. I reassured him that everything was going to be alright and that he was in good hands. I held his hand and sang to him as the IV drip made him drowsy and he fell into a light sleep.

Having had medical issues my whole life, I'm no stranger to surgery, but it was very different being the one sitting nervously in the waiting room, instead of the one asleep, being operated on. I sat in the surgical waiting room for what seemed like days before I was called back to the recovery room. Daniel was groggy, half sitting up in his hospital bed, and was vomiting violently into a bin. I grabbed a nurse and Daniel choked out that the pain medication they were giving him was making him nauseous. I held his hand and calmed him down as they gave him some different pain medication and something for the nausea. He eventually fell asleep and was taken up to his room before I left for the day.

I visited him in the hospital every day after that. A few days after his amputation, Daniel had to have another procedure to remove more tissue from his foot that didn't seem to be healing properly. After that, he had a special type of wound vacuum on his foot and wasn't able to stand up at all for a couple of weeks. Whenever I visited, he would tell me how painful it was to have the wound vacuum changed and his wound cleaned. A couple of times I even held his hand while as they cleaned his wound, which was not pretty to look at. He squeezed my hand so hard it hurt and I would just grit my teeth and try to be there for him. I know he suffered emotionally as well during that time, being stuck in a hospital bed for two weeks straight, so I brought him a little stuffed dog to keep him company when I couldn't be there.

Once his wound started to improve, the physical therapy department at the hospital made sure that he stood up and started walking a little bit with a walker. His mother, stepfather and I all tried to keep his spirits up and encourage him in his therapy and, after three weeks, Daniel was finally able to come back home. His foot, of course, wasn't completely healed by this point. He still had a wound vacuum on his foot and a nurse had to come to the house every day and change his gauze pads and tape, clean his wound, etc. Daniel also still had to have IV antibiotics for a time. We had an IV stand next to our bed and the home health care nurse would also check and change the IV bag daily.

A different home health care aide would come over every day to supervise Daniel's physical therapy. She would work on getting him to stand up straighter, hold on the walker and shuffle along around the house. His walking was getting a little bit stronger every day, which was a good thing. He was eventually fitted with a prosthetic insert that went into his shoe and was supposed to help him walk, but it didn't help too much. Daniel had balance and general walking issues for the rest of his life after his work related accident.

One of the biggest issues, while he was still bed ridden and not permitted to stand up or walk without his home health aide, was using the bathroom. I would clean out the little urinal that the hospital had given us after every time he used it, but getting him next door to the bathroom to do his other business was hard. He would usually have to try and wait to do anything but urinate until a home health care aide or his physical therapist came to the house and could assist and supervise his walking, but my mom and dad helped him walk a few times. Daniel ended up in the hospital again approximately one month after his surgery because he was vomiting so much. He was diagnosed with gastro paresis, which is a condition, often associated with diabetes, where the stomach doesn't empty properly. Because of the gastro paresis, he was in the hospital for three or four days over the Fourth of July holiday. Ending up in the hospital again so soon after his surgery really took its toll on Daniel and we all tried to give him confidence that things would, eventually, return to normal.

One of the worst parts of these post- accident hospital stays was that he had to resign his position with his employer after making a worker's compensation claim for his foot injury. He found a new job very quickly, of course, having the experience in IT that he had. But anyone who knows a diabetic knows that doctors and hospital stays are a regular occurrence, and missed time from work due to injury or illness was an issue for almost as long as I knew Daniel.

He was seen at different walk in clinics and at his primary care physician's office multiple times over the years for headaches, stomach cramps, diarrhea, vomiting, and falling. He was hospitalized at least two more times in the four years after our wedding for gastro paresis, and he was hospitalized twice for injuries resulting from falls around the house. These hospitalizations lasted anywhere from three to five days, and then he'd get to come back home. Unrelated to his diabetes, Daniel also had severe allergy and sinus issues (something we had in common). His allergies were a little more severe than mine, and it seemed like he got sinus infections more often than I did. It also seemed like colds and sinus infections turned into pneumonia rather frequently with him, which didn't tend to happen for me. In the years we were together, he was hospitalized at least two times that I can remember for pneumonia. He was put on oxygen, antibiotics and steroids, and was discharged from the hospital successfully each time.

If you know me, you know that I have always hated hospitals. More than hating hospitals, I have a phobia of them. Even going to my primary care physician's office for a checkup, my heart rate would be elevated.

"Are you nervous?" the nurse would ask.

"No, I'm not nervous, why?"

"Well, your heart rate is very fast!"

"Oh, that's just because I'm in a doctor's office."

"There's no reason to be afraid, dear."

"I know."

While my mind knew that there was no reason to be afraid, my heart didn't seem to fully understand that. I'd feel almost physically ill just walking into a medical facility. Every time Daniel was hospitalized, though, I was there. I didn't normally take him to the walk in clinic or ER myself, but I always made sure to visit at least every other day just to see him. I'd squeeze his hand and tell him I loved him and remind him that he was going to get better. I would text and call him on a daily basis, video calling him with our fat black cat next to me so he could see him too. I am terrified of hospitals, but what I wouldn't give to be able to go to the hospital and see him just one more time.

One of the worst side effects of all Daniel's hospitalizations over the years was that he missed several family vacations that we had previously planned because of injuries or illnesses. Before Daniel and I got together, my parents and I had always tried to take one short vacation

(typically a long weekend in a place within driving distance of home) and one longer vacation (usually a week in a place that we had to fly to) every year. We continued that tradition after we got married. Daniel and I would take a vacation each year by ourselves, and we would take a vacation as a family of four every year as well.

One year we took a boat to Key West, and another year we went to Clearwater to see the Aquarium, all four of us together. Daniel missed a trip to Las Vegas (including a side trip to Kansas City for one of my best friends' weddings) and a trip to Chicago, which really disappointed him. I always made sure to purchase him a baseball cap or a t- shirt from wherever we were visiting, to let him know that I'd missed him and had been thinking of him, but I know it hurt his heart to not be able to go with us to those places.

A few years after we were married, Daniel actually got to go with us to Arizona to visit my grandmother, which was great. He'd never been west of the Mississippi River, and marveled at the red rock and desert landscape of Arizona. We took a day trip from my grandmother's house in Phoenix to Sedona and we got so many beautiful pictures of the area. We didn't have time to visit the Grand Canyon, but we did visit Red Rock State Park and saw the Devil's Footstool. Most importantly, Daniel got to meet my father's mother and brother, which I know was important to us both. I had no idea of this at the time, but that would be our final trip as a family of four before he passed.

5

The Change in Career and the UK

Four years after we got married, I lost my job of six years. That was honestly one of the lowest points of my life. I came home sobbing and Daniel just held me close and reassured me that we would get through this job loss. I was worried that, without the income from my employment as an attorney, we'd never be able to pay our bills. Losing my job, though, actually pushed me to start a new career. Ever since I can remember, it's been my dream to be a children's book author. I love kids, and I love books and combining the two just seemed natural. Daniel encouraged me to write a book and to use some of my savings to pay for its publication.

To celebrate the book that I was going to have published, we scheduled a trip to the UK. It had always been a shared dream of ours to visit England and Scotland but we'd never seemed to have the time and money for it. I found roundtrip airfare and hotel reservations for the both of us for around fifteen hundred dollars total and decided, on a whim, to book it. *You know what,* I thought to myself, *let's just take the leap and go on this trip. We have some savings. Daniel's been rather healthy these past few months and he's got a great job making good money where he can take some time off of work. Let's do this!*

I scheduled a trip from Ft. Lauderdale to London, including a six night hotel stay in London and a day trip to Edinburgh, Scotland to surprise Daniel. He was elated! He informed his employer that he'd need the week off, and I was so excited that I started packing our suitcases two months before we were even scheduled to leave. I researched different activities to do and restaurants to eat at in London and Edinburgh and was so prepared that I even had a whole folder full of maps and information on attractions we'd want to visit. Daniel just laughed at my over planning, but I really think that it was all the planning that made our trip go so smoothly.

On a scorching hot day at the end of May, we set off for the Ft. Lauderdale International Airport for a week in the U.K. We drove to Ft. Lauderdale and stopped at Daniel's brother's house for a brief visit before his brother drove us to the airport and saw us off. To avoid lengthy delays and layovers, I had booked a direct eight hour flight to London and we took British Airways all the way there and back. It was an evening flight, so we got seated on the plane and the stewardess brought us a nice tray of hot food for dinner. We were both surprised at the quality of the food, because it wasn't your typical airline fare. There was a meat dish, some potatoes, a vegetable, and a side of fruit for dessert. We ate up, watched a few episodes of *Game of Thrones* on the screen in front of us, and then I decided to lie down. We were in the middle aisle of the plane, where there were four seats in a row. The two seats beside us were empty, so I lay my legs across the empty seats and Daniel invited me to put my head on his lap and use it as a pillow.

"Are you sure? Don't you want to sleep?" I asked.

He shook his head and smiled at me. "No, I can't sleep on a plane. Go ahead. I'll just lay my seat back and relax a little, but I can't sleep."

I was so excited that it took me forever to fall asleep. When I finally did, I woke up just two hours later. I went to the bathroom quickly and and came back. Daniel was sitting with his seat back and eyes half open, watching a movie that I didn't recognize.

"Not going to sleep?" I asked.

He just shook his head and smiled sleepily.

I lay back down and slept for two more hours.

"What time is it?" I whispered when I saw that Daniel's eyes were open.

"We have two hours left until landing," he whispered back.

I shrugged and sat back up. I couldn't sleep anymore. I popped in my headphones and watched another episode of *Game of Thrones* while Daniel sat back and relaxed with a movie. With just an hour left, the stewardess brought us a hot breakfast. We wolfed down the food and watched out the window as English soil appeared below us. The sun was just coming up. We got off the plane and were both overjoyed that it was actually cool outside.

"Daniel, look! I can wear a sweater!" I exclaimed excitedly, since it had been too hot for a sweater for three months already in Florida. He just laughed.

We were exhausted but we each took a caffeine pill to keep us going as we dragged our luggage out of the airport. We found a ride share and got transportation to our hotel in Central London. I remember watching the English countryside fly by as we drove, and seeing the beautiful yellows and oranges and reds as the sun rose up in the sky. It surprised me that the airport was so far from the city itself, as our ride lasted about forty- five minutes.

We finally made it to our hotel and checked ourselves in. Our room wasn't ready yet but the front desk manager agreed to keep our luggage for us until check in time. She even invited us to partake in the hotel's complimentary breakfast while we waited. We had a full English breakfast almost every day of that trip, including eggs, kippers, back bacon and English muffins.

Daniel had tea, but I stuck with orange juice. After that, we decided to explore London. Using our metro cards that I had purchased while we were in the U.S., we found a tube station about one mile down the road from our hotel. We took the tube to Green Park Station and followed the signs to Green Park and Buckingham Palace. We were your typical tourists, exclaiming over the Palace and taking pictures every two seconds. Daniel noticed that the flag was raised above Buckingham. "Look!" he said. "The queen is in residence!"

I joked that we should knock on the front door and insist that we be allowed to enter, since we were both (distant) cousins of the Queen. We walked through the park, absolutely loving the cooler weather and the shade that all the beautiful trees provided. On the way back to Green Park Station, we stopped at an art museum and admired the paintings of Salvador Dali that were on display. We came across a red telephone booth, and, of course, had to take pictures. After making our way back to the station, we took the tube back towards our hotel. We walked down the road, looking for a restaurant to stop at for dinner before retiring for the night.

We woke up the next morning bright and early. After our full English breakfast, we walked back to the tube station and rode to Westminster. We followed the signs out of the station and found ourselves right across the street from Westminster Palace, also known as the Houses of Parliament. "Look, there's Big Ben!" Daniel pointed out. "They must be doing some type of work on it. See all the scaffolding?" I looked and saw that the entire face of Big Ben was obscured by scaffolding, to the point that it was almost unrecognizable.

We crossed the street and walked around Westminster Palace to the park behind it. Coming upon the river, I exclaimed "The Thames!" We both sat on the wall bordering the Thames River and watched the little boats going up and down the river for a while, just enjoying the mild weather and each other's company. Daniel pointed out the London Eye and the Shard in the distance as he captured video footage of the moment for posterity.

After a while, we continued on to Westminster Abbey, just down the street. We were taking pictures like crazy and lined up with all the other tourists waiting to get in to the Abbey. Luckily, I had previously purchased special passes that got us both in to all the attractions that we wanted to see in London. When our turn came, we showed our passes and were admitted to the Abbey. We marveled at the high ceilings, stained glass windows, and statutes inside. We walked around the Abbey slowly and read each one of the engravings for people interred in the Abbey. Daniel was most excited to find Stephen Hawking's marker, as he had guest lectured one of Daniel's college science classes. I was most excited to see the markers of my Plantagenet ancestors that I'd recently discovered through genealogical research.

The Abbey even had a little place where you could pay two pence to light a candle and say a prayer. Daniel slid two pence into the slot and took a small candle. We lit it, put the candle in the holder, and held hands while we whispered a prayer of thanksgiving that God had allowed us to make this trip, and asking him to bless us and all our loved ones back home. We left the Abbey in a hushed, reverent mood and walked down the street to the Jewel Tower.

We walked around Jewel Tower and then decided to wander around the Westminster area for a while. There was a little pub along the way that looked pretty neat, so we stopped in for dinner and a pint. I had soda, of course, while Daniel tried some of the local beer on tap. He said it was better than American beer, but I'll have to take his word for it. We stopped in a gift shop along the way and purchased souvenirs and made it back to Westminster Station. After riding back to our station, we came across a little ice cream shop. It was quite warm outside that day, by English standards, so we decided to stop and get some ice cream.

Each of us had a chocolate ice cream cone and, while I expected to have to rush back to the hotel so that Daniel could take some insulin after our dessert, his blood sugar remained steady. We asked the server behind the counter why the ice cream tasted even better than it did in the U.S., and they explained that it was homemade and that they didn't use the outrageous amount of sugar in their sweets in the U.K. that they did in the U.S. Daniel was impressed with how much healthier the dessert options were across the pond.

Following our standard U.K. breakfast the next day, we took the tube to Kensington. We strolled through Victoria Park and then toured Kensington Palace. "Maybe we'll see Harry and Meghan!" I cried excitedly. There were no royal sightings that day, unfortunately, but the weather was perfect: sunny and mild. We ate some snacks that I had in my backpack as we sat beside the pond in Victoria Park and we even fed some ducks that were paddling along in the water. We spotted an Englishman walking a Maltese dog through the park and joked that our own dog would absolutely love to walk through the grounds and try to chase the ducks.

Then we decided to try to find the Sherlock Holmes Museum, which Daniel desperately wanted to see. I also wanted to see Scotland Yard, which was supposed to be moderately close to the museum. After a trip on the tube and a hassle filled bus ride to the museum, we found that the museum was not accessible. Daniel was very disappointed, but we stopped along the way at a pizza place and shared a pizza and soda before wandering towards Scotland Yard. We eventually found it, got a bunch of pictures, and then found a tube station to take us back to our hotel. Our intended destination the next day was the Tower of London. After getting our fill of complimentary breakfast, we took the tube to Tower Station. We found our way to the Tower, gained admission with our special passes, and toured the Tower and grounds. Standing in the White Tower, the very place where my sixteenth great grandmother had passed away five hundred years before, was awe inspiring. Walking past Tower Green, where so many people had been executed historically, was rather morbid, but Daniel loved the artillery room and got a lot of pictures of the different cannons. We could even see Tower Bridge in the distance.

After taking the obligatory photo of the two of us with the spires of Tower Bridge in the background, we walked towards the bridge. The sheer size of the bridge and the height of its spires were amazing. We got a million photos of the bridge itself before gaining admission to the top of the bridge with our passes. We toured the top of the bridge, even getting to walk across a section of glass that allowed you to see straight down to the traffic on the bridge and the Thames River below it. Daniel was hesitant to step on the glass, but I even went so far as to lie down on it and take some pictures of myself with the traffic and the river in the background.

Next, we followed the river down to London Bridge. It's a rather plain bridge, we discovered, and when you picture London Bridge in your head, you're probably picturing Tower Bridge. We used our passes to get a tour underneath London Bridge, where we learned the history of London Bridge(s) and even got to see models of each bridge that had existed there since Roman times. After that, we headed towards St. Paul's. St. Paul's Cathedral was one of Daniel's favorite stops of our trip, and I have to admit that it is gorgeous. It's in a beautiful area and the cathedral itself is enormous, with soaring ceilings and beautiful balconies. We got a tour of the cathedral and headed back towards Tower Station. Stopping at a diner for a burger and shake beforehand, we took the tube back towards our hotel.

The next day was one of my absolute favorite days of our entire trip. We got up unusually early, hastily ate our breakfast, and took the tube to Victoria, where we found our way to the coach station. We were just in time to catch the bus to my second home: Warner Brothers Studios in Leavesden! The *Harry Potter* Tour amazed the both of us. From real live set pieces to actual costumes and décor used in the movies, it was a fantastic tour and we both enjoyed a glass of butter beer before heading back on the bus.

"This tastes even better than the butter beer in the U.S.! It's not so sickly sweet!" Daniel exclaimed. I had to agree with him that the U.K. definitely had the U.S. beat when it came to being diabetic friendly.

The day after our *Harry Potter* Studios Tour was, hands down, Daniel's favorite day. We woke up even earlier than the day before (so early we didn't even get breakfast!) and caught a ride share to the airport for our flight to Edinburgh. After checking in and getting on our plane, we had an hour and a half flight before landing on Scottish soil. The moment that we got off the plane, Daniel knelt down on the ground and kissed it.

"I'm home!" he said with tears in his eyes.

After exiting the airport, we found a subway train that would take us in to central Edinburgh. During our short tram ride into the city, we met a kindly young man that offered to show us the way from the central station to Edinburgh Castle. "Everyone here is so friendly!" I whispered to Daniel. "Opening doors for us, asking us if they can help us, and offering to show us how to get to our destinations." He nodded. The British definitely outdid the Americans when it came to kindness.

As our new friend showed us the way from the central subway station to the Royal Mile, he pointed out places of interest to us. He was like a makeshift tour guide, giving us the names and dates of historical events that had happened there and pointing out important locations as he told us about them. Once we hit the Royal Mile, he motioned us towards the Castle and indicated that he was going in the opposite direction. We thanked him profusely and started making our way up the hill. And what a hill it was! When they say that Scotland is hilly, they are definitely not lying. We stopped at a gift shop on the way and purchased souvenirs again. Daniel wanted to stop and buy a kilt, but we didn't get the chance because we only had about eight hours in Scotland. He did purchase a clan tartan scarf, though, from his familial clan.

After puffing our way up the hill, we made it to Edinburgh Castle. It was an immensely old, imposing castle that offered amazing views once you reached the top. The weather was dreary and rainy that day, but we each had ponchos on so we managed to stay (mostly) dry. We made it to the top of the castle and surveyed the landscape. From the top, you could see the sea in the distance, and all of Edinburgh was laid out below you. Daniel pointed out Holyrood Palace and Abbey in the distance, and then insisted that we hit a local pub on the way back to the subway station. At the pub, he ordered haggis and beer for himself and tried to get me to try a bite of the haggis. He thoroughly enjoyed it but I refused to eat it, opting for chicken instead.

All in all, we had around six to eight hours in Edinburgh total. I always wanted to go back to Scotland with Daniel one day, to see Holyrood Palace and Holyrood Abbey, and to visit the Highlands, but it just wasn't meant to be. As we made our way back to the subway station, we came across a bagpipe player in full traditional Scottish garb. He was playing some upbeat music and Daniel and I stopped to listen, even dancing a little bit together when the music called to us. We then got on our plane and headed back to London.

Getting back to London late that night, we took a ride share to the hotel and went to bed. The next morning, we had to get up bright and early and pack our things. We had one last traditional English breakfast before checking out of our hotel and catching a ride share back to the airport. Our flight back to the U.S. was also eight and a half hours, and direct, but it felt like it was a lot longer than that because we were still used to the British time zone.

We had both been taking vitamin C and zinc to try to ward off any illnesses on our trip, but once we got back to Florida, I think the jet lag did us in. We both came down with colds in the week after we returned home and eventually developed sinus infections and had to be on antibiotics and steroids for several days. It took a couple of days to get used to the time change, but we eventually adjusted to Florida time and went back to our usual happy routine as a family for a couple of months until a slip and fall changed our lives forever.

6

The Hospital Again

One Saturday morning in early September, Daniel slipped and fell in our kitchen after accidently dribbling water on the floor as he was preparing his coffee. I was sitting in the family room, eating a bowl of cereal and watching the local morning news when I heard a *thump* and heard him cry out.

I ran into the kitchen. "Oh no! What happened?" I asked.

He was lying on the floor, clutching his knee. "I fell!" Daniel cried. "There was water on the floor!"

"Oh, no," I said. He had fallen a few times in the house over the years. One of those time included hurting his knee cap, so I figured that he had probably injured his knee cap again. I looked at his leg. There were no bones sticking out and he had only a slight scrape on his knee.

"Are you ok? Can you stand?"

"Yeah, I think so," he said.

He stood up with some assistance but he was still grimacing in pain.

"Can you walk?"

"Yes, but it really hurts."

"Do you need to get it looked at?"

"I'll go to the walk in clinic."

My mom and I helped him hobble out of the house and he drove himself to the walk in clinic around the corner. About an hour later he texted me: *It's a broken femur.*

What?!

They're sending me to the ER. Mom is with me.

"Oh, wow. He broke his femur!" I told my mother.

"What?!" she exclaimed. "You can't walk on a broken femur! How was he walking?"

I shook my head in disbelief. "I don't know."

Later that evening, he texted me that the hospital near our house was admitting him and he was going to have to have surgery the next day to repair his femur with pins and screws. I texted him back and let him know that I would be up to see him after his surgery.

True to my word, I went to the hospital the next day to see him. He was worn out from surgery, but they were managing his pain and I think my visit buoyed his spirits. I held his hand, hugged him, and told him I loved him. I visited him a couple of more times after that, as his leg healed. Then, all of a sudden, in the middle of the night one night, approximately four days after he was admitted to the hospital for his broken femur, Diane called me and left me a voicemail saying that Daniel had aspirated on vomit during the night and that the doctors had intubated him and put him on a ventilator after diagnosing him with aspiration pneumonia.

As soon as I got that voicemail, I rushed to the hospital. Daniel was in the ICU in a sedation coma and I sat beside his bed and sang to him and talked to him all morning and afternoon. I even took his cell phone and put on some of our favorite Christian music, leaving the phone beside his head so that he could hear the music, even if he couldn't communicate with us. Daniel slightly woke up once that day, opening his eyes a bit and motioning towards his mouth. He looked terrified when he discovered the tube in his throat, so I tried to calm him.

I squeezed his hand. "It's ok, dear, it's ok. I'm here. You're in the hospital." He took his hand and started to tug at the tube. "No!" I pulled his hand away from the tube and said "No, don't do that. They have you intubated. It's ok. You're ok." He was still motioning towards his mouth and he started to cry. "I know, dear, I know, it's uncomfortable. Don't try to talk. It's ok."

The nurse scurried to his bedside and upped his sedative levels so that he went back to sleep. In the days following that episode, he developed kidney issues and Acute Respiratory Distress Syndrome, which the doctors were very concerned about. It looked quite serious for a couple of days, and I spent the majority of my time sitting beside his bed and praying. Finally, things started to turn around. His chest x- rays were improving and his lab results were looking better. He woke up again while I wasn't there one morning and pulled the tube out of his throat himself before the doctors were completely ready for it to come out.

Diane called to tell me that Daniel was no longer intubated, and I hurried to the hospital to see him. We were all afraid that he would need to be reintubated, but he continued to improve on oxygen and the doctors didn't feel like it was necessary. After a few days in ICU, he was released back to a regular hospital room. A few days after that, disaster struck again. Diane called me and told me that Daniel had a minor heart attack. I rushed to the hospital to discover that they were doing a heart catheterization on him. The results of that test showed that, chemically, Daniel had indeed had a minor heart attack. There were several of his arteries that were severely blocked and he would need three stints placed in his heart to clear them.

He underwent the operation to place the stints the next day and I went to visit him in his room afterwards. Daniel was sitting in his hospital bed, looking depressed. He didn't greet me with his usual relieved smile so I asked him "How are you feeling?"

His eyes filled with tears and he murmured "When they put me under, I saw my dad."

"You saw your dad?"

"Yeah, and it was so great. I miss him so much. I almost didn't want to come back." I started to cry as I clutched his hand.

"Don't ever say that you don't want to come back. You are the strongest man I know, Daniel. If anyone can make it through this, it's you. I'm here for you. I know that you miss your dad. It's natural to miss him. You love him and his passing was so hard. But he's not gone from you." I put my hand to his heart and I said "He's right here." I quoted *Harry Potter* as I smiled through my tears and told him "The ones we love never truly leave us."

That made him smile sadly and I continued "I know it's tempting to stay once you go to heaven. How could you not be tempted? Heaven is perfect. It's like the best vacation, the happiest you've ever been, times a million. It's so great we can't even begin to understand how great it is while we're down here. But you're needed here. Your mom needs you. Your brother needs you." My voice cracked as I said "I need you."

Daniel shook his head. "You don't need me. You could do so much better than me. You could find a guy that's whole, that can hold down a job and not be sick all the time. You could marry a guy that could support you like you deserve."

I shook my head vehemently and sharply said "No. There is no guy that is better than you, do you hear me?" I squeezed his shoulder for emphasis. "No one is perfect. There's, undoubtedly, guys out there that are taller; stronger; objectively better looking." I chuckled and I jokingly added "Less messy. But you know what? None of them can hold a candle to you because you are perfect. You are perfect for me. And that's what matters. I didn't marry Brad Pitt. I didn't marry Bill Gates. I married you. I married you because I love you with all my heart. And no amount of good health, good looks or a fat wallet could ever mean as much to me as you do."

He was crying by this point, and I kissed him softly before giving him a gentle hug.

"I love you, and I always will."

"I love you, too," he murmured.

In total, from the date he was admitted with a broken femur to the time that he was released, he was in the hospital for a month. After that, he still had to go through rehabilitation, which meant that he was in a rehab hospital downtown for an additional month. I visited him at the rehabilitation hospital every other day, as usual, and I even participated in physical therapy with him to try and encourage him in his recovery.

The therapists had Daniel lift arm weights and practice pushing himself up with just his arms from a sitting to a standing position. I had fun doing stretches with Daniel and lifting weights with him. We celebrated our fourth anniversary in the rehab hospital, with me smuggling in some outside snacks and a balloon and card for him. He was released just before Halloween but, unfortunately, he still couldn't come home. Our house wasn't quite accessible enough and he was still non- weight bearing on his bad leg.

Daniel stayed at his mother's house for a whole month while he got home health services for physical and occupational therapy. They worked on slowly getting him up and walking again and, by the end of November, he could walk with a walker again. He had a head cold when Thanksgiving came, so he didn't make it to our annual family gathering, but I video called him from the dinner table to say hello and to let everyone at the table wish him a happy holiday, and his mother made sure to take him lots of leftover turkey and dressing to enjoy.

Early December arrived and Daniel was finally cleared to come back home. December went pretty well, health wise. Daniel was having a lot of pain in his bad leg and had trouble walking or standing for very long, but he managed to get around on his own. He was having migraines a little more often than he had before, which was unusual, but none of us thought anything was really wrong. Daniel had a nagging cough that he jokingly called his "ARDS cough," which his doctor said was to be expected after developing ARDS. We had a happy Christmas gathering at my mother in law's house and Daniel was so happy to be together with all of us. We exchanged gifts and looked forward to another year.

The new year came and Daniel's migraines worsened. One day he started vomiting violently while lying in bed and he made an appointment to be seen by his regular doctor. The doctor examined him and recommended that he go to the ER, because he was afraid that Daniel had had a stroke. He went to the hospital near our house and texted me: *They think I had a stroke.*

I called him back and he was in the ER triage area. Gerry had joined him in the ER and when I spoke with Daniel his speech was somewhat slurred, as if he was drunk. He would repeat himself now and again and his speech was unclear much of the time. They admitted him to the hospital and ran several tests. When I visited Daniel at the hospital the next day, I got a chance to speak with the neurologist, who confirmed that he had a left sided ischemic stroke in his brain, which meant a clotting stroke instead of a bleeding stroke. After some physical, speech and occupational therapy at the hospital and later at a rehab facility, Daniel was pretty much back to normal, although there were times when it would take him a second to remember something. He was out of the house for around one month total after his stroke.

One positive side effect of his hospitalization in January was that Daniel's walking improved as a result of the physical therapy that he received at rehab. He was diagnosed with foot drop and was given these devices that attached to his shoes and pulled his feet up each time he took a step. He was walking as well as he had when I met him! It was amazing to see how well he was doing at physical therapy and that gave him renewed confidence. Once he came back home, we started taking more walks together with our little dog in the evenings and I felt like Daniel was getting stronger, both physically and emotionally.

His stroke also got us talking about death a little bit more, which was definitely not a happy subject but was somewhat therapeutic. We both knew that when we died, our souls would go to heaven to be with the Lord and that we would be reunited with our loved ones that had passed. I told Daniel that, if he died before I did, I didn't want him to come back to me as something random and generic like a butterfly or a cardinal.

"Be a really stand- offish animal, like a cat," I said with tears in my eyes. "Come back as a cat that just comes up to me in the street and stands right in front of me and meows. I'll know it's you."

We also got to discuss any final arrangements that we wanted. Daniel expressed a desire to be cremated, while I wished to be put in a casket. This worked out well, since my parents and I had purchased two side by side mausoleum spots at our local cemetery a few months before and Daniel's urn could be placed in my casket, while "Annie Wagner Palmer" and "Daniel Palmer" could be put on a plate outside of the mausoleum with our dates of birth and death. Although I admonished Daniel that he should continue to fight to stay here on Earth with me, I knew that he would likely pass before I did. I just didn't expect it to be so soon!

7

The COVID 19 Pandemic

We started to hear about COVID 19, or the novel corona virus, in the U.S. sometime in January, I'd say. It first started in China, but I wasn't paying too much attention to any of the news at that time because Daniel was still in the hospital recovering from his stroke. In February, we heard that there was an outbreak of the illness in a nursing home in Seattle where lots of residents became very ill and some even died from it. The nursing home started to forbid visitors from entering the facility but the illness continued to spread to others in the Seattle area. Then it spread to other places in Washington State.

We still weren't too worried about it in Florida. I was still working from home doing legal advising online, Daniel was working from home following his stroke, and my mother and father were both retired by that point, so we really didn't go out of the house all that much. My mom and I ran errands and did the grocery shopping on the weekends. We ate out as a family at a local restaurant once a week. Other than that, though, we pretty much kept to ourselves.

Daniel developed a more severe cough and a runny nose in mid-February. He got me a dozen roses and a little box of chocolates for Valentine's Day, and we had a fantastic dinner at my favorite Italian restaurant, just the two of us. We went for a short drive after dinner, just enjoying the cooler weather as the evening brought lower humidity. We were even wearing matching t- shirts for the romantic holiday. My shirt said "Wifey" and Daniel had a matching one that said "Hubby." Our waitress loved our shirts and even admired the *Harry Potter* type font that they were printed in.

"I had them made a few years ago for our first anniversary," Daniel declared proudly.

Two days later, Sunday, February 16th, Daniel got sick. At first, he just suffered at home, taking over the counter cold and flu medication and trying to rest. Finally, on Monday, he called his primary care doctor and got an appointment because his condition wasn't improving at all. I told him to stay at least six feet away from other patients and if he saw anyone else coughing, he should stay away from them. He texted me from the doctor and told me that he had tested positive for Influenza A.

The next day, Tuesday the 17th, both my dad and I started to feel sick. My mom joined the illness party on Wednesday and we were all coughing, sweating, snotty messes that survived solely on chicken noodle soup and orange juice for the next two weeks. Daniel became so sick on Wednesday the 18th that he had to be taken to the ER by his stepfather, and he was admitted to the hospital closest to our home, diagnosed with pneumonia. He was on oxygen for a few days before being discharged with antiviral medication and steroids.

Unfortunately, because the three of us were still sick at that point, Daniel had to go to his mother's house after he was released. He recuperated there for a week, while we exchanged texts and phone calls and generally tried to get better. On Saturday the 22nd, both my parents and I went to a walk in clinic around the corner because we weren't getting any better. My mom was diagnosed with bronchitis. I tested positive for Influenza A, not surprisingly. My dad was diagnosed with a general respiratory infection. None of us were tested for COVID, so we'll never truly know if we had it at that point, but our symptoms were certainly worse than any flu we'd ever had before. We were all given medication and sent home.

On Friday, February 28th, Daniel called me, crying. His employer had let him go, likely because of all the sick time he had missed from work in the past few months. I tried to comfort him, reminding him of the time that I lost my job and the fact that we had gotten over it. I assured him that he would either find a new full time job, or be able to apply for disability, or work part time. I promised him that we would survive and he didn't need to worry or feel bad about losing his job. By Saturday the 29th, we were all feeling quite a bit better. Daniel came back home, a little more tired and a little more depressed than before, but he came home. He still had a cough, but we thought that was normal, since he'd had ARDS.

It was at this point that COVID 19 started to get really bad. We saw the first cases of it in our city that first week of March, and two people even died from it at the hospital near our house. My mom and I made one final grocery run, stocking up on toilet paper and cleaning supplies so that we could avoid having to go out as much as possible. We all stayed home, as I worked online, my dad sold things online, and my mom cleaned house. Daniel did what he could to contribute around the house and he applied for jobs. I encouraged him to apply to become an advisor with the same company that I worked with, advising on IT issues, and he applied to work online with several other companies as well. He also arranged to apply in person with the Social Security Administration for disability benefits.

Daniel lost his employer provided health coverage in early March and really started to panic. I assured him that he didn't need to worry. If he had some type of episode and ended up needing health insurance, we could apply for emergency Medicaid. We could scrape together the funds necessary so that he could have one month of COBRA coverage. We would find a way to make things work. It was at that time that he made an appointment with a local health insurance representative so that he could obtain coverage for himself through Obamacare. He purchased coverage that would begin on April 1st but, unfortunately, he never got to use it.

It was Sunday, March 15th: The Ides of March. I woke up to Daniel hacking up what sounded like an entire lung and clutching his vomit bucket in the bed beside me. He'd vomited up all of the food that we had for dinner the night before.

"Are you ok?"

"No. I got maybe three hours of sleep. I can't stop coughing!"

My first thought was *Oh, no. It's COVID.*

"Do you need me to call an ambulance?"

"No. Can you call my mom or stepdad to take me to the hospital?"

"Ok."

I called his mother and told her what was going on.

"The hospital won't even let me in the door because of his cough," I said. "We all could be infected with COVID. But you haven't seen him in about a week, so you couldn't be infected."

"Does he have a fever?" she asked.

I handed him the thermometer from the bathroom cupboard and he stuck it under his tongue. His temperature was reading as 98.7 degrees.

"No fever," I said.

"Oh good, it's not COVID," she said. "Gerry is on his way." Gerry came and helped Daniel to the car.

"I'm so sorry about this," he said.

"It's ok, I'm used to it." I chuckled. "It's just our monthly trip to the hospital," I said jokingly.

"We'll go to the hospital around the corner," Gerry said. "It's closer."

"No!" I shrieked. "There are COVID cases there! Go to the one across town."

Using his walker and clutching his vomit bucket, Daniel shuffled out the door behind Gerry.

"I love you, dear," I called as he walked down the front sidewalk. "Let me know what the doctor says!"

How I wish now that I had taken him to the hospital myself! I wish that I had been the one to drive him there, even if only for the extra twenty minutes that I would have gotten with him. But, as they say, hindsight is twenty- twenty, and, unfortunately, I didn't drive him to the hospital. From that point on, my parents and I started to self- isolate at home, fearing that we may have been infected with COVID as well.

As usual, I texted Daniel and asked him: *What did the doctor say?*

Flu is negative, he said.

Oh. Make sure they test you for COVID!

I feel depressed. The doctor has not been back yet.

Don't be depressed, dear. They'll figure out what is going on and get you better soon.

I feel like this is never ending.

I know it's hard, but we'll get through it!

I can't remember the last time I felt good.

Last summer, maybe?

During our trip to London is probably the last time.

You felt good for a while after that, too, up until the leg break. And you'll feel good again, I'm sure of it.

Later, he texted me: *They're keeping me.*

Oh, boy. Are you in an isolation room?

Yes. They think I have COVID.

Did they test you?

Yes. We're waiting for the results.

How long does it take to get the results back?

24 hours.

Oh, ok. Well, you don't have a fever, so let's hope it's not COVID.

He sent me a picture of himself with a big huge oxygen mask over his face.

I love you, dear.

I love you, too. My phone is dying. Call the hospital until I can get my charging cord.

I went to sleep that night praying for his recovery. I texted him the next morning but got no response. I figured that he probably hadn't gotten his charging cord yet, so I called the hospital and they connected me to the nurse's station near his room. She told me that he was still in isolation and that there wasn't really a phone that he could make calls from inside his room but that she would give him the message that I called and that I loved him. Later that same day, on Monday, he texted me and said: *Phone was dead.*

Hi, dear! I've missed you! How are you feeling today?

Like crap.

Are you feeling any better?

Not really.

I'm sorry, dear. The nurse said you were doing better today, at least.

I am trying.

I know, dear. I miss you.

I miss you.

Later, Daniel texted me to say that he was being diagnosed with double pneumonia.

How do they think you got double pneumonia?

They're not sure.

Well, I'm glad to know that you'll be alright. You will be ok, right, dear?

I hope so.

I have faith that you'll be ok. You'll be home with me again soon.

I worked from my computer that day as usual, and then texted him that night: *I love you.*

The next morning, Tuesday the 17th, I got up and got ready for the day. I texted Daniel to say: *Hello dear.*

Hi.

Are you doing any better?

No. Two hours of sleep.

I'm sorry, dear.

I walked the dog with my mother and was then pulling weeds in our front yard when my mother in law called. She told me that they were going to be putting Daniel on a ventilator again because his oxygen levels were getting worse.

Daniel then texted me and said: *Mom will be calling you.*

Just call him, something inside me said. *Hear his voice. Let him hear yours*. I called him.

"Hello?"

"Hi, honey. It's me."

I could hear the hiss and sputter of the ventilator in the background. I could also hear the murmuring and shuffling of nurses in the room. They must have been getting ready to intubate him.

"They're going to put me under," Daniel said quietly. I could tell that he was crying.

"I know, dear. It's going to be ok. You've been on a ventilator before. I know it's not fun, but you'll be asleep. You'll go to sleep, you'll be on the ventilator for a few days, and then you'll wake up and you'll be better."

"I hope so," he whispered.

"I know so," I said forcefully. "We're going to get through this. We always do. I love you."

"I love you, too," his voice broke on the words as he ended the call. Those were the last words that ever spoke to me verbally.

I sat there for a couple of minutes in the front yard, feeling abnormally worried. I usually felt secure that he was receiving top notch medical care and that he would be alright, but something told me to text him again before he went under sedation.

I love you.

I love you more.

Nope.

Yes, I do.

That was the last text that I ever received from him. I knew that he'd received my text because he'd responded, but he never responded to my next text: *Negative.*

After a few minutes, I added: *I love you so much more.*

For the next two days, I called the ICU where he was being cared for two to three times a day. The nurses knew my voice right away and gave me updates on Daniel's condition. Every time I called, it seemed like the same old story: *He's in critical condition. Not getting any better. No medications seemed to be helping.* I asked the nurse several times if I could come up and see him but she said that it would be impossible for me to even get past the front door because Daniel was a possible COVID patient and I may be infected. Hoping that, even if he was unconscious, he could still hear and otherwise sense what was going on around him, I always asked the nurses to tell him that his wife called and that she loved him. I pray that he heard and understood them when they said that and that it brought him some comfort in the end.

On Thursday when I called the ICU, I asked them if his COVID results had come back yet. They told me that the results were just in and they were negative. Fantastic! That meant that I was likely negative too and could go visit him, at least to see him from a distance. I drove to the hospital right away. At the door, I was greeted with a form asking if I had any COVID symptoms. I checked the box for "No." I confirmed that I was there to visit my husband, gave them his name and room number, showed them my ID, and was cleared to go up to the ICU.

I found my way to the area where his room was and found the nurse's station. I introduced myself and asked if I could go in and see my husband. The nurse told me that I couldn't actually go in the room, but if I went around a corner nearby, I could see him. I followed her around the corner and saw a wall of glass. Through the glass, I saw a small hospital room with a single bed and a computer stand next to it. On the bed, Daniel looked like he was asleep. He had the breathing tube down his throat and was hooked up to about a million different machines, blinking and beeping away. There was a nurse in his room, working at the computer. She had on a full gown, gloves, a mask, and a face shield.

The nurse that had showed me to the glass wall tapped on the glass. The nurse inside the room turned her head, nodded at the nurse outside, and stepped out of Daniel's room. A few minutes later, a middle aged nurse wearing only scrubs came out of a room to the side of Daniel's room. She introduced herself. I asked her how Daniel was doing and got the same words all over again. *He's in critical condition. It's very serious. His lungs are bad. His kidneys are shutting down and he isn't putting out any urine.* The nurse also told me that, because of the COVID pandemic, the entire hospital was going to start forbidding all visitors starting in just three hours.

I begged her to see him before the hospital was shut down to visitors, saying that I would put on a gown, a mask, gloves, a full freaking Hazmat suit if I had to, but the nurse said it was impossible. So I sat there for about a half hour, just looking at him through the glass. I watched his chest rise and fall. I watched the machines blink. I memorized every line and every curve of his face. He had grown some stubble while he was in the hospital, and I reminisced about the scratchy feeling of his stubble on my cheeks. How I wished I could just stroke that stubble again. How I wanted to hold his hand and talk to him!

With tears in my eyes, I held my hand up to the glass. "I love you," I whispered. "I'm here, even if you don't know it. Keep fighting, ok? Keep fighting! I'm here for you." I kissed my fingers and held my hand up to the glass again. "I love you." I walked out of the hospital crying, and took a minute to gather myself up in the car before driving home.

On Friday, the hospital called me to get authorization to do a blood transfusion and a bronchoscope. I told the doctor that, if a bronchoscope was what was medically necessary, then they should do it. The doctor then informed me that they were going to send off some of the fluid from the bronchoscope for a second COVID test because all the nurses and the doctors still thought he had it.

"We're throwing everything at him but the kitchen sink," the doctor said. "And he's not improving."

Friday night, the nurse told me that they had just gotten in a special bed to put Daniel on. This bed would allow them to turn him from his back to his stomach and this would, hopefully, help clear his lungs. It also meant, however, that he wouldn't be getting IV nourishment for several days.

"But he's a big guy!" I insisted. "He's tall, and broad. He eats a lot! Is he going to be alright without nourishment?"

"He'll still be getting fluids and electrolytes," she responded. "Don't worry. The human body can go for up to a month without food. The main issue at this point is his lungs. If we continue to give him nourishment while he's on this bed, he may aspirate it into his lungs."

Hesitantly, I went with what the doctors and nurses were saying, and agreed that they should put Daniel on the bed.

Saturday morning dawned and he wasn't doing any better. On Saturday night, he was still no better. On Sunday, I called the hospital and asked the nurse: "If the worst happens and it... it comes time to..." I choked on my words, tears filling my eyes, "to say our goodbyes, would we be allowed to visit?"

"Of course!" she assured me.

Monday morning arrived and we had good news for once. "He's turned a corner!" The doctor exclaimed when I called. He said that Daniel's chest x- rays and his lab results regarding his kidneys were improving. Even better, they were going to try to take him off the ventilator the next day! I rejoiced and sent Daniel a text that I hoped he would get when he woke up.

You're going to be ok! You're going to wake up and be able to text me again!

On Tuesday, I was feeling pretty positive. I went through my normal routine and called the hospital that morning. They told me that he was still doing well. They weren't going to try to take him off the ventilator that day, though, just to be cautious. The nurse indicated that they would try to take him off of it tomorrow. I worked online, cleaned the house, and generally tried to keep busy to keep my mind off of things. I was having dinner with my parents in the family room when I got a call from the hospital.

"Hello?"

"Hello, Mrs. Palmer?"

"Yes, this is she."

"Yes, this is the nurse from the ICU where your husband is. Your husband's heart has stopped and we're trying to revive him."

"Oh, my God, what are you talking about? His heart stopped? But he was doing better!"

"I have to get back in there and help the other nurses. We're doing everything we can. I'll call you back." *Click.*

My dad had muted the television when I picked up the call, and I told my parents what the nurse had said. They both were very concerned but tried to be positive for me. My dad was working on his laptop, and my mom went into the kitchen to clean up after dinner.

I sat there for thirty minutes, shaking and staring at my phone, but it didn't ring. I decided to dial the hospital.

"Hello?"

"Yes, this is Annie Palmer. I'm Daniel Palmer's wife." My voice broke. "His heart stopped and they were working on him?"

"I'm so sorry, ma'am. We were able to get his heart beating again, but every time we got it beating again, it would stop again. I'm so very sorry. We did everything we could, but he didn't make it."

"What?" I croaked. My own heart stopped. My brain shut down. I couldn't breathe.

"He didn't make it," he repeated.

The first stage of grief is denial. "No. No. No!" I screamed, collapsing to the floor.

Clutching the phone to my ear, I kept repeating "No. No. No." I couldn't breathe. *Why can't I breathe? Where is the air? Why can't I get any air?!* "There has to be something more you can do!" I shouted into the phone. "Do something! Bring him back!"

"I am so sorry, ma'am," he murmured.

"He can't be gone! He's only forty- three years old! It can't be true. I don't understand.

He was getting better!" I screamed.

My hand let go of the phone and I just laid there on the carpeted floor, screaming "No!" at the top of my lungs, gasping for breath, sobbing so hard that my whole body shook. My dad got out of his arm chair in a flash and came over to me. He held me and we rocked back and forth as I sobbed and screamed.

My mother came running in from the kitchen and picked up the phone. I didn't hear what she was saying but she started crying too and joined our impromptu group hug on the floor after she hung up the phone. The love of my life was dead. He was gone. I would never see him in this Earthly realm again. *Am I asleep? Is this all just a bad dream? Am I still even alive? Why am I alive? I don't want to be alive!*

I still couldn't breathe. My stomach ached. My chest felt like it was going to explode. *Am I having a heart attack? Can you have a heart attack as a result of grief? Am I having a panic attack? Am I going crazy? Maybe I am. Bring on the strait jacket and the nice, numbing medication to take away this pain. I freaking hate needles, but I don't care, hook me up to an IV drip that will send me off to unconsciousness. I can't live like this. I can't live without him.*

Whenever we had talked about death or heaven or anything like that, I had assumed it would be after we were both old and grey. I mean, sure, he'd be old and grey before I was, since he was ten years older than me. But he couldn't be gone. He just couldn't! He was only forty three! I was only thirty- three! You can't be a widow at thirty- three. Only little old ladies became widows! He wasn't gone. He couldn't be!

The second stage of grief is anger. Anger set in fairly quickly. The doctors and nurses must have given up on him. They must have been so afraid to treat him, afraid that he had COVID that they were negligent and he died. It took them too long to get to him when he coded. They were afraid to be too aggressive with his medication and didn't give him the right dosage. They let him die because he was so medically fragile, with his history of diabetes, heart attack, ARDS, and a stroke. I always hated doctors, and now they had killed my husband.

No, it wasn't the doctors and nurses that killed him. Daniel was the one I should be angry with. He left me. He found heaven and it was so much better than life here on Earth that he stayed, not even caring that it was killing me to be without him. He gave up. I know he did. He figured that, being unemployed and medically fragile and having so many medical bills piling up from a week in ICU that he thought I'd be better off without him. I was angry because I felt like he had reunited with his dad in heaven and didn't want to come back to me. I had always told him that I would never survive the loss of him, but he'd given up anyways.

My anger turned inwards. No, he didn't give up; I killed him. I fussed at him for making messes around the house. *So stupid of me,* I thought, *who the hell cares about a mess on the floor?!* I stressed out too much about bills and made him feel like he was just a paycheck and, once his paycheck went away, he felt worthless. *I told you money didn't make you worthless! I told you that you were more precious to me than any amount of money in the world.* Maybe I killed him by sending him to the wrong hospital. If I would have sent him to the hospital near our house, which had already dealt with COVID, would he still be alive? Later, we would see a news bulletin on television stating that an elderly man died of COVID on the same day and at the same hospital as Daniel, and that this patient had had contact with another patient before his death. Was that "other patient" Daniel? Did the elderly man with COVID have contact with Daniel, and Daniel caught COVID in the hospital and it killed him? Did the hospital kill him? Did I kill him?!

No, Trump killed him. He allowed the virus to come in from China and didn't contain it when it started in Seattle. The government should have shut down the State of Washington to anyone going in or out as soon as it started and COVID would never have even made it to Florida. COVID killed him. Republicans killed him. Trump killed him. We might as well call Trump the Widow maker. *Makes sense,* I thought, *he is a Russian asset and wasn't the Widow maker a Russian submarine?* Yes, I was a Trump widow now. One of Trump's many widows and widowers that would come out of the COVID pandemic in the coming months.

All these thoughts flashed through my mind as I sobbed and was held and rocked by my parents. I looked up and saw our engagement photo on the wall. We looked so young, so happy. And I suddenly felt so old.

"Oh, God," I said. "Diane!" *Had the hospital called his mom to let her know what happened?*

With shaking hands, I picked up my phone again and called her.

"Hello?"

"Mom?" I choked out.

"Yes?"

"He's gone," I said, sobbing.

"Oh, my God," I heard her scream and she must have dropped the phone because I heard a clatter and then Gerry picked up the phone.

"Hello?"

I could hear Diane screaming "My baby!" in the background and I completely lost it. I dropped the phone and sobbed into the carpet, pulling myself into a fetal position. My mom picked up the phone again and let Gerry know what had happened. After about a half hour, my sobs subsided to a quieter crying. My parents managed to get me up off the floor. Mom helped me wash up and get into a pair of pajamas. She gave me a sleeping pill and I cried myself to sleep.

I don't remember much of the next few days. I remember going to a local funeral home and arranging to have Daniel cremated, like he'd wanted. His mom and brother and I agreed on an urn and arranged to have his body taken from the hospital to the funeral home. I requested that his urn remain at home with me until I passed, at which point his urn could be placed in my casket with me and we could be put together in the mausoleum spot that my parents and I had pre- planned for. I remember that a portion of his ashes were going to go to Diane, for her to spread over his father's grave. And a portion of his ashes were going to go with his brother, to be spread in North Carolina in his favorite childhood family vacation spot. I remember that we weren't allowed to have any type of memorial or funeral service until the COVID pandemic passed, but I don't remember many specifics other than that.

Mostly, I remember the hassle with the funeral home. It was a good thing that Daniel had wanted to be cremated because the funeral home didn't want to even touch his body. They wouldn't wash him and wouldn't embalm him for burial. We couldn't even have a final visitation to say goodbye! We finally got the funeral home to agree to let us view his body from a distance in the crematorium before he was cremated. I remember that vividly. My mom led me down a gravel path to a drab cement building. The funeral home director was standing there with another employee. He expressed his condolences. The other employee unzipped a long white bag inside a cardboard box and there he was: my best friend, my rock, my love. His eyes and mouth were closed. He looked so peaceful! It looked like he was just having a restful nights' sleep in our bed. I have no idea why but the iconic lines from the movie *My Girl* just popped into my head: *Where are his glasses? He can't see without his glasses!* I choked out

"That's him." I turned my face into my mother's shoulder and sobbed. "No! It's Daniel. He's really gone!" I sobbed uncontrollably as my mother held me. The funeral home director stood by silently, looking down. I lifted my head. "Can't I touch him?" I asked, moving towards Daniel.

"No," the director said, stepping in front of me. "I'm so sorry, but you can't." I stood there as my mother held me and sobbed for a few more minutes before gulping down my sorrow. I looked at him one last time, trying to burn every last detail into my memory. "I'm not going to say goodbye, dear. We never said goodbye. This is just 'see you later,' ok? I love you. I'll see you later, dear." My mom led me to the car and I cried quietly all the way home.

Other than the funeral home and getting his ashes back, I don't remember much of the week after he passed. I received lots of phone calls, texts, messages, cards, and flowers from family and friends. Everyone gave me their condolences. There were so many condolences. Luckily, I had my mom to help me with the final details because I couldn't have dealt with them on my own. She fielded phone calls, sent thank you cards for the flowers and gifts, went to the bank with me to deal with his bank accounts, called and canceled his cell phone plan and credit cards for me, etc. I had never imagined that there were so many final details to take care of after someone passed away. There was so much sorrow.

That was what I remember most of the two weeks after his passing: sorrow. I had a knot in the pit of my stomach, and a stabbing pain in my heart. Tears were constantly leaking out of my eyes, even when I tried not to think of him. I slept to try to avoid a lot of the sorrow. One week after his passing, it was April 1st and it was time for me to change our bedding. My mom changed it for me but I insisted that she keep his pillow cases on his pillows. They still smelled like him. I sniffed them every morning and every night and told Daniel "Good morning, dear" and "Good night. I love you."

Approximately one week after he passed, I called the hospital to follow up on the results of his second COVID test. The nurse took my information and told me that someone would call me back. Twenty minutes later, the head of ICU called me to let me know that the results were negative.

"Negative? So he didn't have the virus?" I asked.

"Well, not necessarily. We're having a lot of issues with false negatives when it comes to these tests."

"What do you mean false negatives?"

"Even when a person tests negative, they could still have the virus. Statistically, there is a forty to sixty percent chance that, even with a negative result, a person could actually have COVID."

"You mean they can still have the virus, even if they test negative more than once?"

"Yes, they can. All of the doctors and nurses here in the ICU were shocked to find that the results were negative because they all thought that he had it."

"So there's no other way to test whether or not he had COVID?"

"I'm afraid not."

"And there's no way to tell when he got it, if he had it? He had pneumonia in February, was that the start of COVID symptoms and they just got worse in March?"

"No, there isn't any way we can tell when or how a person caught it. I'm so sorry."

I hung up the phone, feeling confused and depressed. I felt like I could never really get any sense of closure until I knew for sure what had caused Daniel's death. But, now that he had been cremated, there were no further tests to be done. His death certificate stated that he died of hospital related double pneumonia, but that was one of the most common causes of COVID deaths. So did Daniel die of double pneumonia that developed because his pneumonia the month before never truly went away, or did he die of COVID? And if he died of COVID, when and where did he catch it? Did he catch it in the hospital in February? Did he catch it in the hospital in March? Had we all had COVID, but my parents and I survived it? To this day, all three of us have aches, pains and the occasional cough that we hadn't had before we got sick in February. The COVID question was a mystery, and we would just have to live with the uncertainty.

Sorrow snuck in when I least expected it. I was going through some of his electronic things, which he had a ton of, and was organizing them to either give them away to a family member or friend that wanted them, or to Goodwill, and I could picture him holding each one of them. I could see him, in my minds' eye, mounting that computer screen, moving that wireless mouse, and running the internet cables behind his desk. He was everywhere.

Three days after he passed, he came to me in a dream. He didn't say anything, he just smiled at me. He was on the other side of a glass wall from me and, when he saw me, he smiled so big. He was so happy. He wasn't leaning on a walker, or stooped over. He wasn't grimacing in pain at all. He wasn't even wearing glasses! He was at peace. He held up his hands, put them together, and curved his fingers into a heart shape like we would do when we sang "Love is an Open Door." And he just smiled at me. Crying, I put my hand up to the glass and suddenly woke up to a soaking wet pillow. I was so angry! Why couldn't I have stayed in the dream with him for just a little while longer?!

The third stage of grief is bargaining. For a few days, I tried to bargain with God. If he would just bring Daniel back to me, just for one minute, I would never say a negative word again. I would sell all my possessions and live on the street after giving the proceeds to charity. I would join a convent! I would do anything if it meant that I could see him just one more time. When that didn't work, I tried to strike a new bargain with God. *If you're going to take Daniel, take me too. Just do it! Give me a heart attack and take me too. I'll do anything if you'll just take me too. You can't leave me here alone!*

The fourth stage of grief is depression. I had been diagnosed with clinical depression at age eighteen and had taken medication for it ever since. The depression brought on by grief was even worse. Because we were still on lockdown due to the pandemic, I had way too much time on my hands to think about Daniel. I had nothing but time to sit around and miss him, to second guess everything and question his death over and over again in my head. I could eat only a little bit before the knot in my stomach made me feel sick. I slept ten to twelve hours a night and was taking naps during the day just to be unconscious for a little while. My parents tried to cheer me up, and tried to get my mind off of things, but the reminders of Daniel were everywhere.

In a way, the reminders were a good thing. Seeing his clothes in the closet, and his razor kit on the bathroom sink almost made it feel like he was going to come home again. But then the realization would hit me like a ton of bricks all over again: he was never coming home. The day that we received his ashes from the funeral home was the very worst. It was so final! I sobbed just thinking of the fact that all that was left of the hands I had held, the face I had kissed, the hair I had rumpled and played with, the arms that had held me, was a pile of ashes. Dust to dust and ashes to ashes. All that was left of the love of my love was ashes. I wanted to dissolve into ashes too, just to be with him.

Several friends and family member reached out to me to express their sympathy in the weeks following Daniel's death, which was definitely comforting. But no matter what I did, it still felt like there was a huge hole in my heart and in my life in general. One day my mother and I were walking our dog around our subdivision. I saw a cat lying under a car in a driveway and bent down to call to it. *Pspspsps.* The cat, surprisingly, trotted down the driveway and came right up to me! *Daniel,* I thought. *You listened to me and came back as a cat!*

"Hello, kitty," I said to it as it walked up to me.

"Meow!" It answered happily.

"Are you a good kitty?"

"Meow!"

I started to pet it after it rubbed up against my leg and tears sprang to my eyes. I felt ridiculous, tearing up while petting a random cat on the street, but I couldn't help but ask:

"Daniel? Is that you? Are you there?"

"Meow!" the cat responded, looking at me intently.

That made me start crying in earnest, of course. "If you're there, Daniel, I love you. And I miss you so much. Thank you for stopping to say hi."

The cat flopped down on the pavement, doing what Daniel and I had called "the lovebug," lying on its back and exposing its belly.

I laughed softly and started to walk away. My mom and our dog were about fifty yards down the road, stopped for my little visit with the cat.

I was sobbing and choked out "It was Daniel! I told him to come back to me as a cat." My mother held me close as I cried on the street. After a few moments I gathered myself together and we started walking down the street. The cat was still standing in the street, staring in our direction. I waved one last time as we went around the corner.

Two days later, we walked by that exact same cat. I bent down, called to it to come to me, and it just stared at me with that typical cat look on its face that says: *Do you think I'm a dog or something? I don't come on command!* That made me think that maybe it really *was* Daniel saying hello when the cat came to me before, because that behavior was just so abnormal for a cat.

One of the most depressing things for me to deal with was the thought of a whole lifetime without Daniel. I've always been a very forward looking type of person. I like to have my future more or less mapped out ahead of time, so not knowing what my life was going to be like ten or twenty years down the road was very difficult for me. What would I be doing? Probably still writing, I guessed. Where would I live? Most likely the same place I lived now. Who would I live with? My parents? I suddenly started to fear that my parents might pass away like Daniel did. What if COVID killed my entire family, but left me behind?! Even if COVID didn't kill anyone else that I knew, my parents were going to die someday; it was simply a fact of life. Statistically, my parents were bound to pass away before I did, leaving me alone. What on Earth would I do without my parents and Daniel? I couldn't make it all alone.

My mom suggested that I may find another husband some day, but the thought of any other romantic relationship was just ridiculous to me. I could never love anyone as much as I had loved Daniel. Daniel was one in a million. There was no way that I could ever find that immediate connection, that spark, that we shared. My dad scoffed at the idea that there was only one person out there for everyone, but I believed it. Sure, there are probably several people out there you could be minimally compatible with, but there's only one soul mate out there for everyone. And Daniel was my soul mate. So, even if I could ever find another guy that was attracted to me romantically (unlikely), and if I could avoid immediately comparing him to Daniel and feeling like I was cheating on Daniel, no other fully grown man would want to live with his in- laws. No one else would be as understanding as Daniel was.

The last stage of grief is acceptance. After a few weeks, I joined a grief support group via video chat. It helped to talk to other people that were grieving, and to speak with a professional counselor about how I was feeling. The very best advice that I ever received was to take things one day at a time. When I woke up in the morning, I would take a deep breath, say "Just one more day" to myself, and go about my daily routine. I forced myself to focus only on what I needed to do that day, nothing more. I would take care of our cats and dog. Clean the house. Do a little bit of legal advising online. Work on my next children's book for a while. Pull some weeds in the garden.

Even though I could no longer go to the gym like I usually did twice a week, I continued to do my daily stretches and sit ups and pushups. I read some books. I used color pencils to decorate some adults coloring books. I made phone calls to keep up with my friends in the Midwest. I even tried to keep in closer touch with my cousins and aunt back in Illinois. At bed time, I would say to myself "I did it. Mark another day off the calendar!" Even though I knew that that one day I was marking off was just one day closer to my own death, it meant one day closer to seeing Daniel, which comforted me.

My parents kept telling me that Daniel would want me to be happy. I supposed that was true, but I found it hard to figure out how to be happy without him. I knew he was in heaven, no doubt, and was whole and happy. But I missed him like hell. My counselor said that feeling was normal, and that it would always be there, but at least it could be manageable. The one thing that I knew for sure was the Daniel would want me to take care of my parents, his mother and stepfather, and his brother and sister in law, niece and nephew, so I did. It helped to feel like I had a job, of sorts, that Daniel needed me to do. I tried to cherish every moment that I had with my parents and our pets. I tried to regularly call or text my in laws to make sure that they were holding up alright during the quarantine.

In the end, I found an acceptance of sorts. I knew that Daniel had loved me fiercely while he was here, and that I had been extremely blessed to have him with me for six of the best years of my life. And, even though I knew that it was always going to hurt to miss him like I did, I knew that he would not want me to give up on life while there were so many people left here for me to take care of. So I started to live for them. I live every day for them, and for Daniel, and I try to avoid thinking about the future too much. I take each day as it comes, and every day that I survive without him is a huge accomplishment.

Once this COVID pandemic is over and it is safe to go outside again, I'll continue to do what I think Daniel would want me to do. I think he would want me to go back to church. He would want me to minister to the little kids and to love on them. I love to travel, and I know that Daniel would want me to keep traveling, and keep seeing new places with my parents and friends. He was so proud of me for publishing my first children's book, and I know he would want me to keep bringing joy to children with my writing. And I know that Daniel will be right beside me the whole way, even if I can't see him. But, for now, while I'm still isolated at home, I'll just keep the love we shared in my heart, and I'll "just keep swimming."

Sarah Fischer Pointer is an attorney and author living in Southwest Florida. In her spare time, she enjoys reading, writing, and traveling.